Writing Local History Today

ABOUT THE SERIES
The American Association for State and Local History Book Series publishes technical and professional information for those who practice and support history, and addresses issues critical to the field of state and local history. To submit a proposal or manuscript to the series, please request proposal guidelines from AASLH headquarters: AASLH Book Series, 1717 Church St., Nashville, Tennessee 37203. Telephone: (615) 320-3203. Fax: (615) 327-9013. Website: www. aaslh.org.

ABOUT THE ORGANIZATION
The American Association for State and Local History (AASLH), a national history organization headquartered in Nashville, TN, provides leadership, service, and support for its members, who preserve and interpret state and local history in order to make the past more meaningful in American society. AASLH is a membership association representing history organizations and the professionals who work in them. AASLH members are leaders in preserving, researching, and interpreting traces of the American past to connect the people, thoughts, and events of yesterday with the creative memories and abiding concerns of people, communities, and our nation today. In addition to sponsorship of this book series, the Association publishes the periodical *History News*, a newsletter, technical leaflets and reports, and other materials; confers prizes and awards in recognition of outstanding achievement in the field; and supports a broad education program and other activities designed to help members work more effectively. To join the organization, go to www.aaslh.org or contact Membership Services, AASLH, 1717 Church St., Nashville, TN 37203.

Writing Local History Today

A Guide to Researching, Publishing, and Marketing Your Book

Thomas A. Mason and J. Kent Calder

ALTAMIRA
PRESS
A division of
ROWMAN & LITTLEFIELD
Lanham • Boulder • New York • Toronto • Plymouth, UK

Published by AltaMira Press
A division of Rowman & Littlefield
4501 Forbes Boulevard, Suite 200, Lanham, Maryland 20706
www.rowman.com

10 Thornbury Road, Plymouth PL6 7PP, United Kingdom

British Library Cataloguing in Publication Information Available

Library of Congress Cataloging-in-Publication Data

Mason, Thomas A.
Writing local history today : a guide to researching, publishing, and marketing your book / Thomas A. Mason and J. Kent Calder.
pages cm.—(American Association for State and Local History)
Includes bibliographical references and index.
ISBN 978-0-7591-1902-4 (cloth : alk. paper)—ISBN 978-0-7591-2395-3 (pbk. : alk. paper)— ISBN 978-0-7591-1904-8 (electronic)
1. Local history—Handbooks, manuals, etc. 2. Local history—Authorship—Handbooks, manuals, etc. 3. LocaL history—Publishing—Handbooks, manuals, etc. I. Calder, J. Kent, 1951– II. Title.
D13.M326 2013
907.2—dc23
2013015986

Printed in the United States of America

To Christine and Tara

Contents

Acknowledgments

We incurred many debts, intellectual and otherwise, while writing this book. Our colleagues on the Editorial Advisory Board of the American Association for State and Local History (AASLH) first encouraged us to undertake this project. Russell Lewis, editor of the AASLH Book Series and executive vice president of the Chicago History Museum, and Bob Beatty, the AASLH's vice president for programs, collegially kept us on task. The AASLH's anonymous outside reader offered some suggestions that enabled us to revise the manuscript in useful ways. Colleagues at the Indiana Historical Society—Ray E. Boomhower, senior editor; M. Teresa Baer, managing editor, Family History Publications; Suzanne Hahn, director of reference services; and Susan Sutton, coordinator, visual reference services; and at Indiana University–Purdue University Indianapolis—Elizabeth Brand Monroe, associate professor of history; Modupe Labode, assistant professor of history and museum studies; and Kristi L. Palmer, associate librarian, pointed out directions for developing the manuscript. Ty Cashion, professor of history at Sam Houston State University, offered useful clarification on divergent strains of Texas history research and writing. Gregory M. Britton, editorial director at Johns Hopkins University Press, contributed his "Why Books Cost: A Quick Lesson in Finance for Publishers," which appears as appendix 8 in this volume. He also read the entire manuscript and offered several suggestions for its improvement. Colleagues at the Rowman & Littlefield Publishing Group guided the book through its writing and publication stages. Marissa Marro Parks, associate editor, advised us as we organized and wrote the manuscript, and Charles Harmon, executive editor, provided needed encouragement at a critical phase of the project. We accept responsibility for the conclusions here presented.

Finally, our wives—Christine H. Guyonneau, university archivist at the University of Indianapolis, and Tara M. Carlisle, librarian at the University of North Texas—helped us to think like archivists and librarians and to realize the expanding range of possibilities for conducting research in the digital age. We therefore dedicate this book to them.

Introduction

People who have cultivated new and detailed knowledge of their locality can perform a notable service by communicating that knowledge. There is great value in researching, synthesizing, and disseminating new knowledge of a community. The writing of local history has expanded its horizons in exciting ways in recent years to embrace culture broadly defined to include a wide variety of topics including music, art, and the social and ethnic composition of the community.

In the introduction to his classic book, *Researching, Writing, and Publishing Local History*, first published in 1976 and last reprinted in 1988, Thomas E. Felt clearly identified his audience: "This book is directed to anyone who has already admitted an interest in studying the past and is now considering doing something about it besides reading the works of other historians."[1] *Writing Local History Today: A Guide to Researching, Publishing, and Marketing Your Book* is intended for the same audience as it exists today.

This book had its origin in a panel discussion in which the authors participated—together with Beth E. Luey, Gregory M. Britton, and Susan Walters Schmid—titled "So You Want to Publish a History Book?" at the 2006 meeting in Phoenix of the American Association for State and Local History. Panelists and audience then recognized that a ninety-minute panel discussion could at most provide only summary introduction to the subject, and that a more detailed and wide-ranging treatment was warranted.

Although many of the interests of today's readers coincide with those for whom Thomas Felt wrote, and much of his advice and wisdom is still valid, the sources for research, the opportunities for dissemination of local history writing, and the economics of book publishing have changed drastically since his book was last reprinted. Thus the Editorial Advisory Board of the American Association for State and Local History, when considering whether another reprint of his book was in order, resolved that instead a thorough update was needed. Nevertheless Felt remains a vital presence in the current work. We have sought to retain a good deal of his organizational structure, much of his advice, and some especially good examples of what William T. Alderson referred to in the original foreword as Felt's "wry humor," which serves to remind us "that we shouldn't take ourselves too seriously as we do our serious work."[2]

The coauthors of this book began working together in the 1980s at the Indiana Historical Society. Thomas A. Mason was named director of publications in 1987; J. Kent Calder began as editor there in 1983. They would work together until 1998, when Calder left to work in the field of college textbook publishing and later served as editorial director at the Wisconsin Historical Society and executive director of the Texas State Historical Association. Mason continued as director of what became the Indiana Historical Society Press until 2006, when he stepped down to resume a career in university teaching. During the time that the two worked together they published many books on Indiana history; founded the illustrated history magazine, *Traces of Indiana and Midwestern History*; and advised and edited many authors working on local history topics. In all their work a primary goal was to broaden the audience for state and local history by presenting sound scholarship written for a general audience in a well-designed form, whether in a book or a magazine article.

"The goal of the author," Tom Mason often explained to local historians aspiring to publication, "is to anticipate every reason an editor might have to say 'no' to your project." To do that, authors needed to be able to put themselves in the editor's place, see their own work as an editor might see it, and understand considerations involving the size of the market for a particular work, the quality of the research and writing, and the amount of effort it would take for a project to be successful. The better an author understands editorial considerations the more likely that author is to be successfully published. This book is intended to help local historians fulfill their publication goals.

Of course, since Felt wrote his book, the world of publishing has changed dramatically. Only a few years ago, few could have imagined how smartphones and tablets, social networking, and cloud computing would change the world. Who could have foreseen in the early 2000s, say, the extent to which e-mail would become the realm of older business people, while the younger crowd extended their social lives and careers in geometric proportions through social networks such as MySpace, Facebook, LinkedIn, and dozens of others? We cannot know with any certainty what technological advancements are on the horizon or measure with any accuracy the effects they are likely to have on society, work, and communication. All we can know is that the pace of change will continue to accelerate, and the impact of those changes for all of us will mushroom.

What does such rapid change mean for those working in the field of local history? On the one hand, it means that there are many more outlets for their work. On the other, it means that they may find it even more difficult to be heard above the din. While the core audience for local historians remains their immediately surrounding community, the new publication landscape allows the work of local historians to be read by the world. Weblogs or blogs, print-on-demand publishing, e-books, and social networks allow dissemination unfettered by the intervention of an editor or a publisher, which places even greater pressure on local historians to do quality work and communicate it effectively. We believe there is a place amid the roar of this technology and information revolution for the local historian. In fact, we contend that an understanding and appreciation of the value of local history is an antidote to many of the ills of information overload that beset us, especially in the realm of an over-abundance of information that is not based on thoughtful examination of sources, solid methodology, and unbiased presentation.

And this is where much of the work of Thomas Felt is still useful. As he explains, there are two essential standards against which the work of the local historian is measured:

> One has to do with ethics, and one has to do with competence. There is an ethical principle common to all good work in history, whether the work be collecting, analyzing, editing, or writing history. It is not just the principle of respect for the truth, but of respect for the whole truth. The distinction is real. It is not enough to avoid lies; the truths that are told must be as complete as the teller can make them.[3]

This "ethical ideal," however, is not a sufficient condition for reliable and readable history. Felt continues with characteristic wryness: "One can have the ethics of a saint and still be an unreliable historian. What more is needed is competence—and that is the proper subject of this book."[4]

Of course, the number of competencies required for successful local history publishing is vast and has only grown since Felt wrote. Added to the nuances and complexities of researching, writing, and traditional publishing is the need for at least a basic understanding of technology and how it is changing the landscape in which the local historian works. This work offers an introduction to these topics and issues, as well as references to other works for more in-depth study. As with the acquisition of any skill, whether it is piano playing or fly-fishing, competence is a matter of study and practice, as well as passion and talent. Felt saw clearly that a "serviceable memory" and a solid "general education" enhance competence. These qualities, building on what he called "a continuing curiosity and alert intelligence," enable a passionate and talented local historian to produce a successful publication.

This book is inspired by all the talented local historians that we have talked to and worked with over the years, and it is written for those like them who already possess the necessary curiosity, intelligence, and passion and are seeking greater competence in crafting their work and disseminating it widely. In the midst of rapid changes in the publishing landscape and the ways that editors and publishers think, it still behooves practicing local historians to think about audience and market in rather traditional ways and to shape their work accordingly. A clear understanding of one's audience will affect the depth of research and style of writing that should be applied, as well as determine the distribution models that are most appropriate for any project.

NOTES

1. Thomas Edward Felt, *Researching, Writing, and Publishing Local History*, 2nd ed. (Nashville, Tenn.: American Association for State and Local History, 1981), xi.
2. Felt, *Researching, Writing, and Publishing Local History*, vii.
3. Felt, *Researching, Writing, and Publishing Local History*, xii.
4. Felt, *Researching, Writing, and Publishing Local History*, xiii.

ONE

The Consumer: Who Is Your Audience?

Identifying an audience is the most fundamental issue that any author or publisher—large or small—must address. "Who is your audience?" should be the first question a researcher/writer/publisher should ask. The answer to that question will determine the medium (printed book or article, website, microform) and level of detail in which the writer will present the results of research. From the nature of your audience, everything else follows in terms of how you communicate your content—the historical subject matter that is the result of your research. The nature of your audience will dictate—if your publication is successful—how your publication is written, designed, formatted (in print or electronically), marketed, and sold or otherwise disseminated.

With each sentence and paragraph, an author must make decisions about what to include and what to leave out, providing enough information so the reader has a proper context for the subject at hand but not so much that the reader becomes lost or bored with information that is commonly known. Only writers who have a good understanding of their audience can make such decisions.

For example, this book is written for a specific audience of those who are passionate about local history and who would like to have a better understanding of the options available for publication of their research. Readers of this book will be involved in researching their family, their community, or a particular topic that interests them, and they would like clues about how to enhance that research and make their writing of it more effective. They will also be seeking a better understanding of the publishing process: how editors and publishers think, and methods for increasing the likelihood that their manuscript or proposal will receive thoughtful consideration rather than no consideration at all. Readers will

1

be interested in at least an introduction to the many ways that the publishing world is changing and the impact of those changes on local history publishing.

This book is not written specifically for students who are working in an academic setting writing research papers and theses. Nor is it written for academic authors seeking to advance their careers by publishing in scholarly journals and academic presses. There are many good books targeted toward these audiences, such as *A Short Guide to Writing about History* by Richard Marius and Melvin Page, *The Information-Literate Historian: A Guide to Research for History Students* by Jenny L. Presnell, and *Handbook for Academic Authors* by Beth Luey. While there is a good deal of information in these books and many others that is pertinent to those writing local history for publication, and while they will be drawn from for this one, such books have not been written specifically for the local historian. This book is.

Potential audiences for local history range widely. Genealogists and family historians write histories of particular families, which they intend for an audience numbering in the hundreds. Authors of such micro-histories often find that the most cost-effective means of publishing their work is to have it duplicated at a quick-print company that can bind the work attractively, and the author can donate the work to family members and local and genealogical libraries. While print-on-demand technology offers new outlets for this kind of work, broad readership is generally not the primary goal of genealogists.

Graduate students often succeed in writing dissertations that meet the standards and expectations of dissertation committees of a half dozen specialist scholars. But recent alumni of graduate programs often face an awakening—if they are lucky, it is an epiphany—when they try to persuade a press to publish a book based on such a dissertation.

An old proverb about graduate education asserts that graduate students learn more and more about less and less until finally they know everything about nothing. A common misconception of first-time authors and neophyte researchers—including students at all levels—is a reluctance to give up or excise from their draft book any minute bit of detail because it took so long to discover during the course of research. The result is a dissertation or book of doorstop weight that few people will read.

If they are going to reach a nonspecialist audience, all authors have to do a crossover of sorts—they must *converge* on their specialized subject, but they must also *diverge* to put that subject in context and provide enough background so it will be intelligible to a nonspecialist audience. Getting that balance right is the great challenge of authorship, and those authors who can do it will succeed and get their work published.

In his significant study of publishing local history, Thomas E. Felt identified five audience groups:

1. "Dedicated and knowledgeable students of your subject . . . never more than a handful."
2. "Adults with a real interest in at least some aspect of your subject" —maybe in the hundreds.
3. "Adults, usually affluent, sharing some interests with members of the last group," but with a more casual interest in history—who would be attracted to well-illustrated coffee-table books—a secondary market—with higher production costs.
4. "A juvenile readership"—to meet educational standards (set by state and federal education authorities)—aimed at school and library sales. The Indiana Historical Society Press has successfully published books for young (middle and high school) readers.
5. "Adults living or working outside the locality or special topic you are describing" —which requires an exemplary study by a sophisticated author.[1]

It is important to distinguish between your audience and the potential universe of people who will be willing to pay for your publication. Those two parts of your market overlap, but they by no means coincide. The Indiana Historical Society Press learned to its sorrow that the number of people who would actually pay for printed copies of conference proceedings—no matter how important to the historical field—or research tools such as cumulative indexes for historical periodicals is negligible. But when we put such publications on our website, they received tens of thousands of page views, even before they were announced, marketed, or advertised. Cases such as indexes and conference proceedings demonstrate in the starkest terms the contrast between mission fulfillment and cost recovery.

What are your options for reaching your audience—be it a book-buying audience or an audience of Web users who expect to get their information for free? The good news for authors and historical organizations is that it is easier to get published in some form today than ever before. The advent of electronic publishing has broadened the options for authors and historical organizations and revolutionized the publishing industry.

The more sobering news is that the specialized monograph that used to be the bread and butter of historical societies and university presses is much less tenable than it used to be. Specialized monographs now sell 200 or 300 copies if the publisher is lucky—numbers at which it is impossible to recover production cost. As a result, historical societies and university presses are seeking "mid-list" titles that will appeal to a more general, nonspecialist audience. The specialized monograph is clearly beleaguered but can be viable in the right circumstances. Publishers with title lists in specialized subject areas such as military history, especially the Civil War, and museum publishers with title lists focusing on art history—and the knowledge of how to market to their subject areas—can successfully market such monographs.

Identifying the audience (market) for your publication is the first task for the researcher, writer, and publisher, and communicating with that audience about the publication (marketing) is the final task. The nature of the audience will drive the shape and characteristics of your publication. If the audience is "dedicated and knowledgeable students of your subject . . . never more than a handful"—Felt's category 1—then your publication can go to extended length and into minute detail, but you should consider a photocopied or Web-based publication, not a printed book, the production of which would be cost ineffective. If the audience is primarily "adults with a real interest in at least some aspect of your subject" or a more casual interest in history—Felt's categories 2 and 3—then your publication can be of short or medium length and can go into some detail on the subject, always subordinating detail to a role of illustrating and substantiating the broad argument, interpretation, and narrative of the book. Once the nature of the audience has shaped the characteristics of the publication, and you have researched, written, and produced it, then you and your publisher will be ready to market your publication (topics discussed in the following chapters).

To justify the expense of a book in the twenty-first century, you need to have a potential book-buying public—not just an audience—of several thousand. Throughout the publishing industry, only about 7 percent of all book titles, and about 5 percent of self-published book titles, sell more than a thousand copies.[2] While new media in various formats, including all forms of social media, provide a wide range of alternative delivery systems for historical content and may bring that content to many more individuals, the writing still may not justify the investment and risk that is the key to any book project and to understanding the thinking of editors and publishers.

How then do editors and publishers think? Who are the audiences they have in mind? One of the most important books for any author wading into the waters of local history publishing and wanting to understand its range of motives is Carol Kammen's *On Doing Local History*. In it she provides a summary of local history's publishing past that is useful for understanding where such publishing is today. Defining local history as "the study of past events, or of people or groups, in a given geographic area . . . based on a wide variety of documentary evidence and placed in a comparative context that should be both regional and national," Kammen explains that, despite its narrow geographical concerns, it is nevertheless a "broad field of inquiry," encompassing political, economic, and cultural concerns, or at least it should be.[3] She identifies the practice of local history as primarily within the purview of amateurs and acknowledging the gulf that often exists between the local historians working in their communities and the professional historians working in academia.

The author then puts her finger squarely on an issue that has great significance for the publishing prospects of any work in local history, and it is one with which the local historian must come to terms in order to enhance those prospects.

Local history publishing has its roots in a time when there was little or no distinction between the work of amateur and professional historians and when even the best of these authors infused their work with myth and boosterism in order to celebrate a community, establish its superiority, and perhaps encourage immigration. Kammen quotes historian John Higham in calling these authors, mostly men, "patrician historians." What they shared, she says, was "some measure of education and an interest in writing essays about their hometowns."[4] These are the kind of men who founded the Indiana Historical Society in 1830, as one example, within the generation following statehood. That society defined its mission or "objects" of "the collection of all materials calculated to shed light on the natural, civil, and political history of Indiana, the promotion of useful knowledge and the friendly and profitable intercourse of such citizens of the state as are disposed to promote the aforesaid objects." These "objects" and the language in which they are expressed reflect a patrician attitude or ideal that would be the norm as leading men formed historical societies and associations throughout the country in the nineteenth century.

The Indiana Historical Society met only twelve times between its founding in 1830 and its revitalization in 1886, when—according to former director Peter T. Harstad—a group of "lawyers, writers, professional historians, editors, librarians, and Hoosiers from many walks of life gradually transformed a state-chartered corporation that received a few small appropriations from the General Assembly into a multifaceted, privately financed twentieth-century institution."[5] Two aspects of this statement are particularly noteworthy. One is that by the 1880s the patricians of the early nineteenth century were giving way in the local history realm to what Kammen has called "members of the nascent professional class whose occupations allowed them the leisure to engage in the writing of history" and whose writing was primarily commemorative, promotional, or filiopietistic. The other is the emergence in the late nineteenth century of the "professional historian," and at that point the purposes of and audiences for local history began to diverge in ways that remain significant for today's practitioners.

This divergence, however, did not fully manifest itself for some time. The goals and perspectives of the academic and nonacademic historians coincided in the beginning so that they found common ground in collecting and publishing important foundational documents, establishing journals such as the *Indiana Magazine of History*, and providing necessary funding to make the partnership viable. Kammen recounts the story of Johns Hopkins University professor Herbert Baxter Adams's efforts to encourage his graduate students to work on local topics and to further collaboration between "the local cultural establishment and the emerging professoriate." He helped to found the American Historical Association (AHA) in 1884 as a means to facilitate cooperation. "It was his intention," writes Kammen, "that the new association include gentleman scholars as well as professionals and that the AHA would provide direction for local historical societies."[6] Adams's intentions for the AHA were not fulfilled. The professionals showed little respect for what some considered buffs and dabblers. As a result, both amateurs and specialists felt snubbed. Several specialist organizations—the Society of American Archivists in 1936, the American Association for State and Local History in 1940, and the Association for Documentary Editing in 1978—spun off from the AHA when their members concluded that the AHA was not serving their interests. Herbert Baxter Adams's dream of cooperation, though not realized by the AHA, persisted in the state and local historical organizations that formed around the country.

Other than the historical societies and associations, the most important publishers were commercial entities that created a successful formula that consisted of engaging agents, or "compilers," to solicit contributions from prominent individuals and families and asking them to pay a fee to be included in a proposed volume of local (usually county) history. The process not only funded the manufacturing of the volume, but it also included a built-in distribution mechanism through family and business networks, taking a good deal of the risk out of the publishing venture. Anyone who does research in the field is familiar with these volumes and with the kind of material they offered. Regardless of the location, the story that emerged was the same for all. Kammen refers to Indiana folklorist Richard Dorson's *American Folklore and the Historian* (1971) to explain:

> They began with a reference to Indians and the wilderness topography; hailed the first settlers; noted the first churches, the first schools, the first stores; . . . swung into full stride with the establishment of the newspaper, the militia, the fire department, and the waterworks; . . . recounted the prominent citizens of the community, and enumerated famous personages . . . who had passed through; listed a roster of Civil War dead; and rounded off the saga with descriptions of the newest edifices on Main Street.[7]

This is not a bad description of what even today's academic historians think about the worst characteristics of local history writing and publishing, but these volumes are invaluable for researchers.

This successful publishing formula declined as the forces of modernization in the twentieth century such as automobiles, new roles for women, and a more international focus derived from World War I became prevalent. As Kammen states, "Nothing could have been more old-fashioned, more passé, more out of date than local history."[8] Local history writing and publishing nevertheless continued, supported primarily by historical societies and commercial publishers who could figure out how to make it pay, and the best way to make it pay was to continue in the celebratory vein and to ignore the impact of significant changes taking place in the world. Academic historians increasingly sought to work with the growing number of university presses, which in the beginning received significant support from their institutional hosts to further scholarly discourse. The scholarly presses had a greater impact in serving the tenure and promotion needs of the academics than local commercial publishers or historical societies, and at this point the divergence of the two modes of writing and publishing local history became pronounced.

Texas offers a particularly revealing landscape for studying the diverging strains of state and local history writing. This is not only because many books are published on Texas history each year by a wide range of publishers, but also because Texas is a place where the hold of a particular romantic interpretation of history continues stubbornly to survive despite the efforts of a couple of generations of academic historians to revise it, temper it, and encourage it to evolve in ways that reflect the conditions and inhabitants of a state that is rapidly changing.

Historian Walter L. Buenger, professor at Texas A&M University and former president of the Texas State Historical Association, has worked for many years on defining the various approaches to Texas history and interpretations of Texas identity, along with their ramifications for publishing. He is among a number of historians who have identified a particularly resilient traditionalist approach in which little attention is paid to women, and non-Anglo populations are generally not considered as worthy or capable of controlling Texas. While such attitudes have been tempered since the 1960s, the traditionalist approach depicting a time when "sundrenched white men strode nobly into the frontier," is still strong and reflects a desire to retain traditional values and identity in a state that is rapidly growing more diverse and more urban.[9]

A proponent of historian C. Vann Woodward's belief that the "shelf life" of any version of historical truth should be limited to no more than a generation, Buenger maintained in "The Shelf Life of Truth in Texas," the introduction to the edited volume *Texas through Time: Evolving Interpretations* (1991), that the Lone Star State was holding on to earlier historical constructions that centered around the Texas Revolution, the Civil War, and frontier conquest longer because they, wittingly or unwittingly, "underscored uniqueness, justified racism and other prejudices, and confirmed political ideology." By 2011, when his follow-up essay "Three Truths in Texas" appeared as the introduction to the anthology *Beyond Texas through Time: Breaking Away from Past Interpretations*, Buenger acknowledged that the competing historical interpretations of traditionalism and revisionism had evolved into three truths that moved in "a multilinear fashion," that is "three evolving, sustained, and only partially connected ways of seeing the past." These were what he calls "updated traditionalists," "persistent revisionists," and a third interpretation that he labels "cultural constructionists." Updated traditionalists celebrate and preserve the accomplishments and influence of leaders in business, politics, and military affairs, and their work provides moral lessons for today's readers. Persistent revisionists are intent on broadening the definition of who is a Texan from the perspectives of gender, class, and race. While they have done great service creating a more inclusive story of Texas, they often depict such minority groups as Mexican Americans, African Americans, and Indians, as victims rather than as "agents of their own fate." Cultural constructionists, according to Buenger, examine the interactions between cultural groups at specific places and times, especially those that involve conflict. They are writing for a national audience of historians in an effort to "cross the spatial and intellectual borders of Texas and Texas history."[10]

The point of this discussion for local historians generally is not that one form of writing is necessarily better or more publishable than another (though Buenger, as an academic, is definitely in favor of the cultural constructionist approach). The point for us is rather that such varieties of approaches to history writing exist, that they appeal to different audiences and publishers, and that an awareness of them and where one's work falls within them will help local historians communicate with editors and find the publisher that is right for them.

According to Buenger, more than 1,600 first edition books were published on Texas history between 1988 and 2009. Of that number, he categorized 45 percent as "updated traditionalist," 46 percent as "persistent revisionist," and 9 percent as "cultural constructionist." The kinds of presses that brought out these books broke down as follows: 14 percent came from university presses outside of Texas; 28 percent were published by the two primary university presses in the state, University of Texas Press and Texas A&M University Press; 25 percent were brought out by not-for-profit Texas presses; and 33 percent of the books were published by commercial presses. Significantly, University of Texas Press and Texas A&M University Press published books in all three of Buenger's interpretive categories.

Buenger found that the number of books published on Texas history, as well as the number of publishers bringing out those books, increased each year during the two decades, despite the many changes taking place in the book publishing industry and some dire predictions about its future. Publishers in Texas and elsewhere took advantage of marketing opportunities provided by the Internet, efficiencies made available by print-on-demand technologies, and the economies of less expensive foreign manufacturing to enhance sales and control costs. As a result, says Buenger, "the book trade experienced a democratization that allowed almost anyone with a story to tell a chance to tell it."[11]

Traditionalists' efforts to celebrate and commemorate the past were aided by a rapidly growing population of newcomers that was interested in learning about and taking part in the Texas mystique, a society changing rapidly and yearning for the comfort of a simpler past, and the celebration of the fiftieth anniversary of World War II and its accompanying adoration of the "Greatest Generation." With the changing roles of women in sports, business, and politics and the growing influence of the Mexican American population, the traditionalists became more inclusive in the ongoing celebration of significant individuals.

For local historians, such developments provide greater opportunities for publication and distribution. Declining institutional support over the past twenty years has led many university presses into what is called regional trade publishing; that is publishing books about a particular region in the realms of history, geography, environment, music, and art that will appeal to an audience in the thousands rather than in the hundreds, the distribution of the average scholarly book. Authors wanting to submit a book to a university press should be aware of similar books on the list, able to describe how their project fits into the list and will enhance it, and have a good sense of exactly who the book is intended to reach (as in Felt's descriptions above), and specific ideas about how to get information about the books to that audience. Authors with a track record who bring a viable marketing plan to the table and are willing to play a major role in implementing it will attract the attention of editors at smaller university and not-for-profit presses. Most presses will have guidelines for authors on their website, and some will provide a form for providing necessary information about a project. Authors will be asked to suggest possible readers for the press's review process, and, as the process moves forward, may be asked to help find financial support, or a subvention, for a book, especially if it involves photographs or artwork that may be expensive to procure or reproduce.

In addition to the regional publishing efforts of university presses, a number of commercial local history publishers have come into being over the last couple of decades that specialize in providing books for niche audiences. These presses, such as Arcadia Publishing, founded in 1993, and the History Press, begun in 2004, have found ways to work with organizations and communities to publish projects that reach a general audience and are financially viable. Driven by passion for preserving and commemorating the past and taking advantage of new technology, such presses have played a major role in the increase in local history publishing in the last twenty years. According to its website, "Arcadia has blended a visionary management approach with the innovative application of state-of-the-art technology to create high-quality historical publications in small local niches." It has eight thousand books in print and releases hundreds of new titles each year. It is best known for its Images of America series that "celebrates a town or region, bringing to life the people, places, and events that define the community" primarily through historical photographs. It also has series on sports, railroads, aviation, postcards, business, and schools. The site boasts a new series started in 2011, Legendary Locals.[12]

Likewise, the History Press has found a formula for making local history publishing profitable. The mission of the press, as stated on its website, is to preserve and enrich community

> by empowering history enthusiasts to write local stories for local audiences. Our books are useful resources for research and preservation, but it is their value as touchstones for community identity that drives us to publish works that national houses and university presses too often have ignored. Infused with local color, our books are highly readable, often brief and aimed at a general readership.

The guidelines for authors encourage prospective authors to spend time with the catalog and become familiar with the twenty or so series offered by the press, including American Heritage, American Legends, Brief History, Definitive History, Disaster, Forgotten Tales, Vintage Images, Sports, and Wicked. The publishers say that they are also willing to consider projects outside the series "so long as the story is inherently local and there is an identifiable community that will relate to the work." Also, in what is good advice for pitching to any publisher, the guidelines state, "the more thorough your proposal is, the more seriously it will be considered."[13]

Presses like Arcadia Publishing and the History Press, producing books in the traditional vein, help to account for the continuing increase in local history publishing that Buenger noted in his study of Texas publishing, and they provide new options for those working seriously on local history topics.[14] These books do not necessarily move the dialogue between traditionalists and revisionists forward, and they are not meant to since that is primarily an academic exercise. Instead, they should move forward the kind of goals ascribed generally to local historical societies by Anne W. Ackerson in her entry for the *Encyclopedia of Local History* (2nd ed.) on "Connection, Civic Engagement, and Collaboration." Publications done well can connect people to the past, engage communities, and build partnerships that maximize the value and reach of a shared understanding of the connections between the past and the future.[15]

Thus, the climate for local history publishing is a good one, with many options available. Nevertheless, those who best understand the motives of publishers, the needs of their audience, and methods of communicating their research will have the greatest chance for success.

NOTES

1. Thomas E. Felt, *Researching, Writing, and Publishing Local History*, 2nd ed. (Nashville, Tenn.: American Association for State and Local History, 1981), 64–66. Felt was senior historian at the New York State Education Department.

2. Tony Cook, "Self-Publishing Comes in from the Cold with Sale," *Indianapolis Star*, July 20, 2012, A-5.

3. Carol Kammen, *On Doing Local History*, 2nd ed. (Walnut Creek, Calif.: AltaMira Press, 2003), 4–6.

4. Kammen, *On Doing Local History*, 12.

5. David J. Bodenhamer and Robert G. Barrows, eds., *The Encyclopedia of Indianapolis* (Bloomington: Indiana University Press, 1994), 739–40.

6. Kammen, *On Doing Local History*, 20–21.

7. Kammen, *On Doing Local History*, 26.

8. Kammen, *On Doing Local History*, 27.

9. Walter L. Buenger and Arnoldo De León, eds., *Beyond Texas through Time: Breaking Away from Past Interpretations*, new ed., twentieth anniversary ed. (College Station: Texas A&M University Press, 2011), 7–8.

10. Buenger and De León, *Beyond Texas through Time*, 3.

11. Buenger and De León, *Beyond Texas through Time*, 32.

12. "Arcadia Publishing Series—Imprints, Arcadia Publishing," n.d., www.arcadiapublishing.com/series.html.

13. "About The History Press," n.d., http://historypress.net/about-hp.

14. Buenger found that 33 percent of the 1,600 books about Texas published between 1988 and 2009 came from commercial presses, and these commercial local history presses originated during the period of the study with strong Texas lists (Buenger and De León, eds., *Beyond Texas through Time*, 7–8). Similar growth in local history titles nationwide can be inferred from the Texas information.

15. Carol Kammen and Amy H. Wilson, eds., *Encyclopedia of Local History*, 2nd ed. (Lanham, Md.: AltaMira Press, 2012), 323.

TWO

Evidence: Where Do You Find It? How Do You Use It? (Research)

The general principles of research have remained constant, while the media and the procedures necessary to extract information from those media have altered fundamentally. Legal historians learn that the connection between law and history is evidence: Where do you find it and how do you use it? Historians of the ancient world (from which relatively few documents survive) learn that documents and artifacts alone are not evidence. They do not speak for themselves. The evidence is derived from the questions that are asked of these sources. Thus, researchers who know the right questions to ask will be successful in turning documents and artifacts into evidence that is revealing and useful for understanding the past.

Computers and the Internet have revolutionized the research process. The researcher should combine the best of both worlds—print and electronic media—in accessing source materials. In the electronic age as in the age of print, the researcher's most valuable ally remains the reference librarian. Excellent general introductions to research techniques include:

- Jacques Barzun and Henry F. Graf, *The Modern Researcher* (1957; 6th ed., Belmont, Calif.: Thomson/Wadsworth Publishing, 2004). It is no coincidence that this guide has been in print for more than half a century and has gone through six editions.
- David R. Beasley, *Beasley's Guide to Library Research* (Toronto: University of Toronto Press, 2000).
- David E. Kyvig and Myron A. Marty, *Nearby History: Exploring the Past around You* (1982; 3rd ed., Lanham, Md.: AltaMira Press, 2010). This book provides an excellent introduction to the variety of evidence available for the study of local history and guidance on how

13

to deploy it. See especially chapter 2: "What Can Be Done Nearby?" (the questions to ask when constructing a local history), pages 17–43; and chapter 3: "Traces and Storytelling" (how to structure and construct a local history, and where and how to find evidence), pages 45–60.

- Thomas Mann, *The Oxford Guide to Library Research* (1987; 3rd ed., New York: Oxford University Press, 2005).
- Jenny L. Presnell, *The Information Literate Historian: A Guide to Research for History Students* (2007; 2nd ed., New York: Oxford University Press, 2013).

Historians recognize two fundamental categories of source materials. Primary sources include original records and eyewitness accounts such as government documents, diaries, letters, images of various kinds, interviews, e-mails, blogs, and social media. Secondary sources include interpretive works written after the events they describe, such as journal articles, specialized monographs, encyclopedias, biographies, obituaries, and surveys of local, state, national, and international history. Secondary sources are based on primary sources and incorporate, in varying degrees, narrative and analytical elements. Autobiographies, newspaper articles, and radio and television broadcasts can serve as either primary or secondary sources depending on the questions that are asked of them and the context in which they are used.

HOW TO ANALYZE EVIDENCE

When analyzing any historical document or book, regardless of whether it is in print or in manuscript, found online or in a library or archive, the researcher should address/answer the following questions:

- Who wrote this document or book? Who was the author (if known)? What were the author's personality/character/circumstances/rank/office/relationship with the intended audience/recipient? These characteristics of the writer will provide insights into why he or she wrote the document or book.
- Where (location) and when (date, as exact as possible, approximate if necessary) was the document or book created? The place/setting where the author wrote the document or book can provide an insight into his or her motivation and concerns.
- What audience/recipient did the author intend to reach with the document or book? Public? Private? In the case of a book, within the general reading audience that any author of a published book intends to reach, what specific/core audience did the author hope to reach with this book?

- Was the document or book commissioned? If so, who commissioned it? Private or public patron? Governmental entity? Religious organization? It is important to know the context of the commissioned work since the commission might reveal some bias, influence, deference to the patron, or other limitation, whether deliberate or unintentional.
- What does the document or book tell us about the society in which it was created?
- What was the author's purpose in writing the document or book? To put it another way: Where is the author coming from? Where is he or she going with this document or book?
- How well did the author achieve that purpose?
- What are the document or book's strengths and weaknesses?
- To what extent did the author set standards for accuracy in writing history?
- To what extent are the author's expectations and standards of accuracy similar to or different from modern/current standards?
- To what extent have modern/current expectations and standards of accuracy changed since the author's time?
- How did the author deal with the challenges and dilemmas that he or she encountered?

Not all evidence appears in the form of books and manuscripts. Be sure to consider the evidence provided by material culture: archaeology, art, architecture, historical geography, environment, monuments, cemeteries, tombstones, and their inscriptions. When analyzing an artifact as historical evidence, the questions you should ask are variations on those used in analyzing a document or book:

- Who created the artifact? Who was the creator/artist/craftsman (if known)?
- Where and when (date, as exact as possible, approximate if necessary) was the artifact created?
- In what medium was the artifact created? Painting (oil, tempera, watercolor, fresco)? Sculpture (bronze, marble, terracotta)? Drawing (graphite, print, engraving, etching, pastel)? Mosaic? Textile? Furniture (wood, metal, other material)? Photograph?
- What was the intended audience/use for the artifact? Public? Private?
- Was the artifact commissioned? If so, who commissioned it? Private or public patron? Governmental entity? Religious organization?
- If the artifact is a work of art, what is its subject? Portrait (individual, group, self-portrait)? A religious subject (representation of a scriptural or devotional subject)? Historical (a major subject area since the sixteenth century has been history painting)? Domestic (northern European artists from the fifteenth century, and

American painters since the nineteenth century, specialized in domestic scenes)? Landscape? Townscape? Seascape?

- What does the artifact tell us about the society in which it was created?
- If the artifact is a work of art or useful, is it realistic or idealized? Is it characteristic of an identifiable style?[1]

RESEARCH

With those guidelines about how to analyze historical evidence in mind, you are now prepared to search for that evidence.

An extraordinary range of primary source and secondary source materials is available on the Internet, with more being added each day. Still, what is available online is only a fraction of what can be found in physical repositories. Digital collections can lead researchers to much greater riches in archives, libraries, and museums, and these institutions in turn will often have digital collection guides (also known as finding aids) that can be examined in advance to help researchers plan how to make a visit as productive as possible.

Searching for historical materials on the Internet involves a good deal more than just firing up a web browser of some kind, such as Explorer, Safari, or Firefox, and conducting a keyword search through a search engine such as Google or Bing. Doing so can provide tens of thousands of results, but if the searcher does not have at least a rudimentary understanding of how search engines such as Google or Bing work and some searching skills, those results are not likely to be very helpful.

Search engines match a search request with keywords and web pages and then post the results with URLs (or uniform resource locators), which serve as the address of a website. The leading search engines use sophisticated algorithms to find websites, but such sophistication does not mean that the most relevant sites will appear at the top of the search results list. A website may be ranked higher because it is more popular, though it may not have the most useful or trustworthy content. Analyzing a website's address, as well as its content, is a necessary step in evaluating its value as a historical resource.

A URL uniquely describes how to access a specific online resource. URLs typically have the following format: protocol://computer .domain.name/pathname/file.

A domain name consists of a string of identifiers that defines a particular realm of administrative authority and control on the Internet. It is very important that researchers pay attention to domain names when evaluating search results. The most prominent top level domain names are *.com* (commercial), *.edu* (education), *.gov* (government), and *.org* (organization). Academic websites, including academic libraries, use *.edu* and can generally be trusted to provide more authoritative historical information than *.com* or *.org*, though exceptions abound. Many historical organizations use the .org domain name, including the Wisconsin Historical Society at www.wisconsinhistory.org, the Virginia Historical Society at www.vahistorical.org, and the Texas State Historical Association at www.tshaonline.org. It is the mission of historical organizations like these to provide easily accessible and trustworthy information, and they can be counted on to do so. But not all organizations are equally trustworthy. Researchers should maintain a certain amount of skepticism regarding the intentions of an organization and the information on its site. websites using the domain *.org* can have political or ideological axes to grind, and researchers should evaluate those intentions with the same care they would those of a historical document or photograph.

In a world in which blogging has begun to take the place of accurate journalism and in which historical analogies, often spurious or fabricated, are used to justify political and commercial ends, how is one to trust that the quotation or interpretation of events their browser has landed them on is worthy of being included in their work and passed on? Providers with apparent intellectual or political biases must be screened out.

For example, the Institute for Historical Review (IHR; www.ihr.org) claims the following as its mission:

> The Institute for Historical Review is an independent educational research and publishing center that works to promote peace, understanding and justice through greater public awareness of the past, and especially socially-politically relevant aspects of twentieth-century history. We strive in particular to increase understanding of the causes, nature and consequences of war and conflict. We vigorously defend freedom of speech and freedom of historical inquiry.

Nothing is wrong with this mission on the face of it until one reads a little further that "we have come under fire from hostile sectarian groups that regard the IHR as harmful to their interests. Zionist groups such as the Simon Wiesenthal Center and the Anti-Defamation League routinely smear the IHR, attacking us as a 'hate group' or dismissing us as a 'Holocaust denial' organization."[2] Upon reading such a statement, the researcher is obligated to question the veracity or academic integrity of any information found on the site.

Researchers can often begin with trusted websites that provide lists and links to other trusted websites. The Library of Congress (LOC) offers many of these. Its "American Memory" project (http://memory.loc.gov/ammem/index.html) is the longest running and most extensive digital collection in the country, providing "free and open access through the Internet to written and spoken words, sound recordings, still and moving images, prints, maps, and sheet music that document the American experience. It is a digital record of American history and creativity."[3] The materials are from the collections of the Library of Congress and other institutions, and they reflect historical events, people, places, and ideas that are integral to American history. Launched in 1994 as the leading effort of the National Digital Library program, "American Memory" surpassed the Library's goal of providing access to five million items by 2000. Offering the ability to browse and search by collection, topics, time period, and types of materials, "American Memory" is a critical place to begin research for almost any local history project dealing with the United States.

From the "American Memory" site researchers can link to other useful sites for primary historical materials, including the Library of Congress's "Primary Sources by State" and "State Resource Guides." Among these sites is one of the best places to begin looking for local history materials on the Internet: the LOC's "State Digital Resources: Memory Projects, Online Encyclopedias, Historical & Cultural Materials Collections" (www.loc.gov/rr/program/bib/statememory). Compiled by Christine A. Pruzin, the site features an exhaustive list of digital projects from museums, libraries, archives, and historical organizations throughout the country. These projects, inspired by the American Memory project, "provide unprecedented access to materials that document local and regional growth and development as well as a look at the cultures and traditions that have made individual states and communities unique."[4] This site is a state-by-state listing of digital archives, such as the California Digital Archive, Alaska's Digital Archives, the Virginia Memory project, the Portal to Texas History, and many more, which digitize holdings of repositories in their states and make primary source materials available to researchers. Also included in these listings are digital encyclopedias that provide signed and vetted articles on states and regions. These encyclopedias, led by early efforts such as *The Encyclopedia of Cleveland History* (http://ech.cwru.edu, 1998) and the *Handbook of Texas Online* (www.tshaonline.org/handbook/online, 1999) have been followed by other ambitious initiatives, including the *Tennessee Encyclopedia of History and Culture* (http://tennesseeencyclopedia.net, 2002), *HistoryLink.org: The Free Online Encyclopedia of Washington State History* (www.historylink.org, 2003), *The New Georgia Encyclopedia* (www.georgiaencyclopedia.org/nge/Home.jsp, 2004), and the online version of the *Encyclopedia of Chicago* (www.encyclopedia.chicagohistory.org, 2005). They are indispensable guides to local history information that can open up directions for further research through their links and bibliographic references.

Many reference works are now online, but some of the best-quality reference works—peer-reviewed sources such as the *American National Biography* and the *Encyclopædia Britannica*—are proprietary publications whose websites require a paid license or must be accessed through the network of a licensed institution such as a participating public or university library. In 2012 the *Encyclopædia Britannica*—first published in 1768—

ceased to publish its print edition and is now available only online (www.britannica.com), surely a landmark in publishing history.

DATABASES OF PRIMARY SOURCES AND SECONDARY INTERPRETIVE WORKS

During the 1990s commercial publishers of scholarly journals (especially in the sciences) escalated subscription prices. The serials crisis of that decade triggered a "crisis in scholarly communication"—serials unit costs went up by 135.56 percent, forcing libraries to increase their serials budgets by 109.6 percent.[5] In an effort to circumvent this price gouging, university libraries, university presses, and nonprofit publishers formed consortia, began publishing journals online, and established databases that are accessible by subscription and by students, faculty, alumni, and community residents affiliated with institutional subscribers.

In 1993 the Johns Hopkins University Press and the Milton S. Eisenhower Library at the Johns Hopkins University founded Project MUSE (http://muse.jhu.edu; subscription required), an online database containing peer-reviewed academic journals and electronic books funded by the National Endowment for the Humanities and the Andrew W. Mellon Foundation. As a nonprofit collaboration between libraries and publishers, Project MUSE expanded in 2000 to include journals and e-books published by other academic publishers. The database now provides access to more than 550 journals and 23,000 e-books in the humanities and the social sciences from 200 university presses and scholarly societies. This database, like those described below, requires a subscription but may be accessible through academic or public libraries if the researcher is affiliated with the library.

In 1995 William G. Bowen, the former president of Princeton University, founded JSTOR (short for Journal Storage; www.jstor.org) with support from the Andrew W. Mellon Foundation. JSTOR is a digital library that provides access to 237 current and more than 1,500 archival scholarly journals, primary sources, and more than 15,000 scholarly books.

In her entry for the *Encyclopedia of Local History*, "Local History Resources Online," Virginia Cole lists a number of databases, or "collections of information stored electronically and now usually accessed through the World Wide Web" that are indispensable for historical research. "Many of the most powerful and largest databases," she explains, "are produced by commercial firms and require subscription for access."[6] Among the sources she cites are the following:

- America: History and Life (www.ebscohost.com/academic/america-history-and-life; subscription required) is a full-text database that indexes 1,700 journals dating from 1910, books, dissertations, and citations and links to book and media reviews relating to state, provincial, and local history of the United States and Canada. America: History and Life is run by EBSCO Publishing, an Ipswich, Massachusetts-based aggregator of full-text content.

- Google Scholar (http://scholar.google.com) is a bibliographic database and web search engine that indexes journal articles and books. In most cases the user can only access an abstract (when an article or book is still copyrighted) and can access the full text only through a licensed institution or by payment of a fee.
- Google Books (http://books.google.com) is an online book search engine. The user can search the full text of the more than twenty million public domain books and magazines that Google has scanned. The user can have only limited access to books and magazines that are still copyrighted.

OPEN ACCESS VERSUS PROPRIETARY SOURCES

Open access is the latest trend that is challenging university presses and other publishers of scholarly books and journals. Open access is a mode of publishing by which the user gains free and unrestricted access through the Internet to peer-reviewed scholarly journal articles. It is also being extended to books, theses, and dissertations. But university presses and journal publishers still more or less operate in the market economy — they recover their costs through sales and subscriptions; most history journals require subscriptions or licenses to gain access to online editions. These licenses are available through most academic and many public libraries if the researcher has an affiliation with the library.

The Directory of Open Access Journals (www.doaj.org) provides free full-text access to a multitude of scholarly and scientific journals available only online. It "aims to be comprehensive and cover all open access scientific and scholarly journals that use a quality control system to guarantee the content." The contents of these journals will not be included in standard periodical indexes or be accessible from Internet search engines. This is a "one stop shop" for users of open access journals, containing thousands of academic journals from around the world.[7]

Since Jimmy Wales, Larry Sanger, and others founded *Wikipedia* (http://en.wikipedia.org) in 2001, it has become a mainstay and first stop for students, journalists, and researchers. Instead of peer review, *Wikipedia* relies on crowdsourcing (with some oversight by an editorial staff) and a gift economy. Crowdsourcing has a long history, going back to the *Oxford English Dictionary*, work on which began in 1857. But in 2006 Jeff Howe coined the term to mean "taking a function once performed by employees and outsourcing it to an undefined (and generally large) network of people in the form of an open call. This can take the form of peer-production (when the job is performed collaboratively), but is also often undertaken by sole individuals. The crucial prerequisite is the use of the open call format and the large network of potential laborers."[8]

Users have free access to *Wikipedia*, which receives financial support from donations to the Wikimedia Foundation. As in any publishing venture, the *Wikipedia* editors wrestle with issues of accuracy, interpretation, and context, and in the process, *Wikipedia* has become increasingly reliable during the past decade. A *Wikipedia* article's source list, if provided, may offer suggestions for further research.

Because of the extraordinarily large size of *Wikipedia*'s audience—its "United States" article alone received twenty million page views during 2011—major cultural and educational institutions such as the National Archives, the Smithsonian Institution, and the Indiana Historical Society have initiated a new form of quality control known as "open authority." These institutions regard it as part of their mission to assure the accuracy of *Wikipedia* articles by providing the services of Wikipedians in residence—personnel (usually working off budget on soft-money grants) on the staffs of these institutions who write and check the accuracy and sources of articles in their fields of expertise.[9] Nevertheless, *Wikipedia* as a cited source still carries less credibility than the digital proprietary encyclopedias mentioned above, and researchers should be wary in using its articles as evidence in their research.

Many additional databases of primary sources and secondary interpretive works, relevant for historical research in general and local history in particular, are available. Museums and university, college, and public libraries often host websites and databases on the history and primary sources (documents, visual materials, and artifacts) relating to their locality. For more information, the researcher should consult a librarian, who can help to differentiate between free and proprietary online sources.

PRIMARY SOURCES FOR LOCAL HISTORY

Most repositories in the general categories listed below have collections including manuscripts, journals, and books. Documents, and the evidence they provide for local history, can be found in:

- City and county courthouses (for land records [deeds, mortgages, and assessed valuations], probate records [wills, estate inventories, and ademptions], tax records, marriage and divorce records, civil and criminal court proceedings, and trial records [order books and case files]). Some city and county courts have turned over their historical records to state archives. For a helpful guide to research, see James D. Folts, "court records," in Carol Kammen and Amy H. Wilson, eds., *Encyclopedia of Local History* (2000; 2nd ed., Lanham, Md.: AltaMira Press, 2013), 120–27.

- City and county health departments (for records of births and deaths). Some city and county health departments will give only transcripts, not copies of original birth and death certificates. Some county health departments will release such certificates only to family members. In some states, the state health department issues death certificates. Before the twentieth century, churches maintained such vital records (of births [baptisms] and deaths [burials]).
- City and county public libraries often have a local history or special collections room that includes books, manuscripts, maps, and photographs relating to the locality.
- Local and county historical societies have special collections of books, manuscripts, maps, and photographs relating to the locality. These societies and their collections are often housed in local public libraries.
- State historical societies (for special collections of books, journals, manuscripts, maps, and photographs relating to the state). Some state historical societies are state agencies; some are independent membership organizations; others are public-private partnerships.
- State libraries (for special collections of books, journals, manuscripts, maps, and photographs relating to the state).
- State archives (for government documents, often manuscripts, generated by state agencies). Many state archives also include collections of private papers among their collections, as well as centralized holdings of city and county records no longer in everyday use.
- The National Archives and Records Administration (NARA; www.archives.gov). Prominent record groups that can be useful to local history include military, personnel, and pension records; land claims; federal court records (including bankruptcies); passenger lists; naturalization records; and census records. The National Archives has repositories in downtown Washington, D.C. (Archives I); College Park, Maryland (Archives II); twenty regional archives throughout the United States; and thirteen presidential libraries. See *Guide to Federal Records in the National Archives of the United States*, Robert B. Matchette, comp., 3 vols. (1974; 3rd ed., Washington, D.C.: NARA, 1995), also available at www.archives.gov/research/guide-fed-records, which contains the most up-to-date information. See also Loretto Dennis Szucs and Sandra Hargreaves Luebking, *The Archives: A Guide to the National Archives Field Branches* (Salt Lake City, Utah: Ancestry Publishing, 1988) and *Guide to Genealogical Research in the National Archives* (1982; 3rd ed., Washington, D.C.: National Archives and Records Administration, 2000).
- Independent research libraries have special collections of books, manuscripts, maps, photographs, and historical prints that are useful for researching state and local history. The Newberry Library

(www.newberry.org) in Chicago has outstanding collections on American Indian and indigenous studies, Chicago and the Midwest, and genealogy and local history. The American Antiquarian Society (www.americanantiquarian.org) in Worcester, Massachusetts, has particularly strong collections (many of which are digitized) of American newspapers and engravings, and the history of printing. The Huntington Library (www.huntington.org) in San Marino, California, has collections of books, manuscripts, maps, photographs, and historical prints relating to American colonial history, eighteenth-century American military history, the American Revolution, the Civil War, the exploration and development of the American West, the building of the transcontinental railroad, and California from its discovery to the present. The William L. Clements Library (www.clements.umich.edu) at the University of Michigan has major collections for the study of early exploration and settlement of North America, the American Revolution, the American Civil War, African American history, Native American history, race and ethnicity, reform movements, religion, and women's history.

Useful directories of all the above-mentioned categories of repositories include:

- *Where to Write for Vital Records*, published by the Centers for Disease Control's National Center for Health Statistics (www.cdc.gov/nchs/w2w.htm).
- Alice Eicholz, ed., *Red Book: American State, County, and Town Sources* (1992; 3rd ed., Provo, Utah: Ancestry Publishing, 2004).
- *American Library Directory*, 2 vols. (1923; 65th ed., Medford, N.J.: Information Today, 2012).
- *Subject Collections: A Guide to Special Book Collections and Subject Emphases as Reported by University, College, Public, and Special Libraries and Museums in the United States and Canada*, compiled by Lee Ash and William G. Miller, 2 vols. (1958; 7th ed., New Providence, N.J.: R. R. Bowker, 1993).
- *Directory of Special Libraries and Information Centers: A Guide to More Than 37,500 Special Libraries, Research Libraries, Information Centers, Archives, and Data Centers Maintained by Government Agencies*, edited by Matthew Miskelly, 1 vol. in 6 parts (1963; 40th ed., Detroit, Mich.: Gale/Cengage Learning, 2012).
- *Directory of History Departments, Historical Organizations, and Historians* (1976; 34th ed., Washington, D.C.: American Historical Association, 2008; since then published online at www.historians.org/pubs/directory2). The section on historical organizations (limited to institutional members of the American Historical Association) in-

cludes historical societies, archives, and historically related research libraries.

- *Directory of Historical Organizations in the United States and Canada*
  (1986; 15th ed., Walnut Creek, Calif.: AltaMira Press, 2002); published for the American Association for State and Local History.
  Many of the organizations listed (limited to institutional members
  of the American Association for State and Local History) are libraries, historical societies, and archives with collections of archives
  and books.
- Philip M. Hamer, *A Guide to Archives and Manuscripts in the United
  States* (New Haven: Yale University Press, 1961); compiled for the
  National Historical Records Commission.
- Repositories of Primary Sources (www.uidaho.edu/special-
  collections/Other.Repositories.html): Terry Abraham of the University of Idaho Library compiled this list of links to more than five
  thousand "websites describing holdings of manuscripts, archives,
  rare books, historical photographs, and other primary sources for
  the research scholar." Coverage is worldwide but is especially detailed for the United States and Canada.

The following directories are searchable online at Archive Finder
(archives.chadwyck.com; subscription required):

- *Directory of Archives and Manuscript Repositories in the United States*
  (1978; 2nd ed., Phoenix: Oryx Press, 1988); published for the National Historical Publications and Records Commission; contains
  information on more than 5,600 repositories and 175,000 collections
  of primary source material in the United States.
- *National Union Catalog of Manuscript Collections* (NUCMC), 35 vols.
  (Ann Arbor, Mich.: J. W. Edwards, 1959–1993); since then also
  searchable on the Library of Congress website (www.loc.gov/coll/
  nucmc); contains more than 115,000 records.
- *National Inventory of Documentary Sources in the United States* (NIDS-
  US) (Teaneck, N.J.: Chadwyck-Healey, 1983–); published for the
  Manuscript Division Library of Congress; also searchable at www.
  proquest.com/en-US/catalogs/collections/detail/National-Inventory
  -of-Documentary-Sources-in-the-United-States-260.shtml; subscription required; provides a complete indexing of more than 72,000
  collections. Academic and many public libraries give access to the
  ProQuest database and other databases to researchers who are affiliated with those libraries.

Search engines can be used to locate source materials in several media.
Bibliographical databases such as the Online Computer Library Center
(OCLC)—which merged in 2006 with the Research Libraries Information
Network (RLIN)—can be searched by author, title, and subject and pro-

vide access to books, manuscript collections, and other media. OCLC can be accessed publicly through www.worldcat.org; WorldCat is a union catalog that provides access to collections in 72,000 libraries in 170 countries. It can also be accessed through proprietary databases, which require a license and password, FirstSearch (www.oclc.org/firstsearch), or OCLC Connexion (connexion.oclc.org). Academic and some public libraries give access to these databases to researchers who are affiliated with those libraries.

Most libraries and archives now have online catalogs; manuscript repositories provide online access to many collection guides and other finding aids. A collection guide describes a manuscript collection and how it is organized and provides a list of containers, boxes, and folders. When conducting manuscript research in an archive, the researcher should examine in advance any collection guides available—whether in print or online—to prepare ahead of the visit to maximize the productivity of the researcher's time when there. Special collections (which include categories such as manuscripts, rare books, and visual collections such as prints and photographs) do not circulate—you have to consult them on site. Always let the archives staff know in advance that you are coming and the topic you are working on—archivists sometimes have the desired materials pulled from the stacks and available for the researcher upon arrival. Always bring a photo identification with you; most archives and special collections welcome public researchers but will require you to register and provide identification on your first visit. Be prepared to use a pencil, not a pen, when taking notes; most archives and special collections also now allow the use of a personal computer for taking notes. Some archives and special collections also allow the use of a camera or cell phone to take photographs. Again, remember that the researcher's best ally is always a knowledgeable reference librarian or archivist.

Despite the widespread availability of online catalogs, collection guides, and finding aids, the researcher still must master the printed subject area bibliographies. A good place to start is Frank Freidel and Richard K. Showman, *Harvard Guide to American History*, 2 vols. (1896; revised ed., Cambridge, Mass.: Belknap Press of Harvard University Press, 1974). Volume 1 is organized topically, including a comprehensive section on biography; volume 2 is organized chronologically.

Another useful resource is *The American Historical Association's Guide to Historical Literature*, general editor, Mary Beth Norton, associate editor, Pamela Gerardi, 2 vols. (1927; 3rd ed., New York: Oxford University Press, 1995), particularly the following sections (all in volume 2): Section 39: Jack P. Greene, "Colonial North America," pages 1239–79; Section 40: Lewis Perry, "United States, General," pages 1280–323; Section 41: David L. Ammerman, "American Revolution and Early Republic, 1754–1815," pages 1324–60; Section 42: Thomas Dublin, "United States, 1815–1877," pages 1361–411; Section 43: Joe W. Trotter, "United States, 1877–1920," pages 1412–52; Section 44: James T. Patterson, "United States History since 1920," pages 1453–503; and Section 45: John M. Bumstead, "Canada," pages 1504–46.

TAKING NOTES

Once you have located the primary and secondary sources for your project, you will need to compile research notes. As you conduct your research in those sources, you will need to take notes, from which you will write the narrative of your publication. Tips on note taking:

- Learn to be selective—learn how to summarize in your own words. You can quote verbatim only a tiny fraction of the material on which you take notes. Thus you must learn to identify those revealing passages that are truly quotable, summarize the rest, and accurately record the full bibliographical citation in the notes (so when you reach the writing stage of your project, you can easily cite your source without having to return to it for the details). If the desired end product is an article or book, it is ultimately more efficient to take accurate summary notes than to photocopy reams of documents.
- Manuscripts and printed materials are subject to copyright laws. It is a researcher and author's responsibility to learn how much (actually how little) he or she can quote verbatim in the finished book. Thus it is important to learn how to take summary notes, summarize details in the narrative, and quote sparingly—reserving verbatim quotations to the most telling and illustrative examples. In short, researchers and authors must learn how to shape the material with the end product constantly in mind. (See discussion of copyright and the concept of "fair use" in chapter 3.)
- A researcher must beware the fallacy that vast amounts of scanning, photographing, or photocopying equal research. Those who photocopy large numbers of documents and never seem to bring their writing projects to a conclusion are not researchers; so do not confuse verbatim copying (scanning, photographing, or photocopying) with research.
- Clearly demarcate within quotation marks material that is copied verbatim, to avoid inadvertent plagiarism later. (See discussion of plagiarism in chapter 3.)
- When quoting from primary sources or secondary interpretive works, always retain the original spelling, capitalization, and punctuation in your notes. Verbatim transcription is generally no impediment for modern readers, and you will need to state in the introduction to your publication if you have modernized your transcription of historical documents.

- Indicate deletions from quoted material by using an ellipsis: ". . .". Use an ellipsis of four periods when ending a sentence.
- Use [*sic*] to indicate a recognized error in the original sparingly.
- Be cautious in assuming that you know more about your subject than the eyewitnesses who lived through the events that they and you are describing.

REFERENCE MANAGEMENT SOFTWARE

Numerous online bibliographic tools can aid researchers in managing research documents, notes, and references. For those of us who learned to store notes and bibliographies on index cards, the workings of this kind of software can seem almost like magic. Among the most popular are EndNote, RefWorks, and Zotero. All of them streamline workflow by easily capturing bibliographic information from online library catalogs, bookselling sites, newspapers, blogs, and web pages with just a mouse click. The programs can store this information and manage it in numerous ways, such as easily inserting references into the text while you write and formatting bibliographies to accommodate the common citation conventions. They can also store notes, documents, and image files to accompany each source. Most, like EndNote and RefWorks, cost money, but those working through an academic library with a license may have access to them for free. Zotero is an open source tool created by the Roy Rosenzweig Center for History and New Media at George Mason University. It is available for free and works with the Firefox web browser and with just a little practice can become an indispensable tool for any researcher.

GENEALOGICAL AND FAMILY HISTORY RESEARCH

In recent decades, genealogy and family history have converged and cross-fertilized with social history to produce some remarkable publications. At the Indiana Historical Society, *The Hoosier Genealogist*—published quarterly from 1961 to 2005 and containing mostly lists abstracted from records—transformed in 2006 into *The Hoosier Genealogist: Connections*, which provides narrative articles placing the records in their social context. This recent synthesis of genealogy and family history has resulted in *Finding Indiana Ancestors: A Guide to Historical Research*, edited by M. Teresa Baer and Geneil Breeze (Indianapolis: Indiana Historical Society Press, 2007). The essays in this book—on topics such as Internet research, oral history, photographs, and maps—range far beyond the borders of Indiana and are applicable to American family history research generally. Chapters on categories of records including census records, church records, court records, and cemeteries are particularly helpful. Another basic introduction to the field is Val D. Greenwood's *The Researcher's Guide to American Genealogy* (1973; 3rd ed., Baltimore: Genealogical Publishing Company, 2000).

Two associations have played important roles in establishing standards for the field of genealogy. The National Genealogical Society (3108 Columbia Pike, Suite 300, Arlington, Virginia 22204-4370; local phone (703) 525-0050; toll-free phone (800) 473-0060; fax (703) 525-0052; www.ngsgenealogy.org) sets high standards for research, evidence, and documentation. The Federation of Genealogical Societies (P.O. Box 200940, Austin, Texas 78720-0940; phone (888) 347-1500; fax (866) 347-1350; info@fgs.org; www.fgs.org) provides institutional developmental services to local and state historical and genealogical societies.

Several major databases are useful for genealogical research (at academic and some public libraries, researchers can gain free access to the proprietary databases requiring subscription if the researcher is affiliated with those libraries). Those databases include:

- PERSI (Periodical Source Index) provides searchers with access to historical information in more than three million local history and genealogical articles appearing in more than ten thousand periodicals published by local, state, national, and international societies and organizations. Indexed by the staff of the Genealogy Center at the Allen County Public Library in Fort Wayne, Indiana (the second-largest genealogical library in the United States), PERSI is the largest subject index to genealogical and historical periodical articles in the world. Accessible through the websites of the Family History Library, HeritageQuest Online, Ancestry.com, Cyndi's List, and the Allen County Public Library.

- The Family History Library at the Genealogical Society of Utah (the largest genealogical library in the United States), 50 East North Temple, Salt Lake City, Utah 84150-9001; (801) 538-2978; The Family History Library website (https://familysearch.org/archives) provides step-by-step instructions on how to conduct family history research. The Family History Library, operated by the Church of Jesus Christ of Latter-day Saints (LDS Church), operates seventeen regional and thousands of local (ward, branch, and stake) Family History Centers throughout the United States and other countries.

- HeritageQuest Online (www.heritagequestonline.com/hqoweb/library/do/index; subscription required) enables searches in census, birth, death, marriage, and divorce records, as well as passport and military pension application files, passenger lists, PERSI, books, and other records.

- Ancestry.com (www.ancestry.com; subscription required): Developed as a publisher in electronic formats during the 1990s, Ancestry.com is now an Internet company based in Provo, Utah. The company provides access to more than ten billion genealogical and historical records.

- Cyndi's List (www.cyndislist.com; free) provides access to a list of more than 325,000 links in 192 categories to genealogical and historical research websites.
- The USGenWeb Project (www.usgenweb.org): Volunteers compile this project, which contains links to genealogical websites in every state and county in the United States.
- Linkpendium (www.linkpendium.com) also provides links to more than ten million genealogical websites in all states and counties.

Several broad categories of records relevant as evidence for local history include:

NEWSPAPERS

From the colonial period, newspapers provide a detailed insight into the daily life, economy, and politics of local communities. Newspapers were the primary forum for debate on political issues. They recorded elections and the proceedings of colonial assemblies, state legislatures, and Congress. Historical and modern newspapers are available in microform and online. An essential guide to research in early newspapers is Clarence S. Brigham, *Bibliography of American Newspapers, 1690–1820*, 18 vols. (Worcester, Mass.: American Antiquarian Society, 1913–1928). Major databases providing access to historical newspapers include:

- Chronicling America (http://chroniclingamerica.loc.gov) is the best place for a researcher to find information about historical newspapers and select digitized newspapers. Produced by the National Digital Newspaper Program (NDNP), a collaboration of the National Endowment for the Humanities (NEH) and the Library of Congress (LOC), this rich digital resource is permanently maintained at the Library of Congress.
- America's Historical Newspapers (www.newsbank.com/readex/? content=96; subscription required): The most comprehensive available collection, America's Historical Newspapers includes digital copies of thousands of newspaper titles from all fifty states published since 1690. It draws on the collections of more than ninety major newspaper repositories including the American Antiquarian Society, the Library of Congress, and the Wisconsin Historical Society.
- ProQuest Historical Newspapers (www.proquest.com/en-US/catalogs/databases/detail/pq-hist-news.shtml; subscription required): A subsidiary of ProQuest LLC, an Ann Arbor, Michigan-based publisher in microform and electronic media, it provides ag-

gregated databases including thirty-nine ProQuest Historical Newspapers—mass-circulation newspapers published in the United States (thirty-three, including nine African American and four American Jewish titles), and one each from Canada, England, Scotland, Ireland, Israel, and India.

CITY DIRECTORIES

The larger cities of the colonial and early national periods had directories that researchers can use to locate persons, businesses, and institutions. A researcher can identify directories through Dorothea N. Spear, *Bibliography of American Directories through 1860* (Worcester, Mass.: American Antiquarian Society, 1961).

RELIGIOUS RECORDS

Before counties and states began keeping vital records (of births, marriages, and deaths) about a century ago, religious organizations— churches and synagogues—were the primary recorders of births (baptisms), marriages, and deaths (burials). To access these records effectively, the researcher must understand the administrative units and structures (congregations, parishes, presbyteries, dioceses, etc.) that generated these records. For a helpful introduction to the field of local religious history, see James P. Wind, *Places of Worship: Exploring Their History* (Nearby History Series; Nashville, Tenn.: American Association for State and Local History, 1990) and James D. Folts, "Religion in North America and Its Communities," in Carol Kammen and Amy H. Wilson, eds., *Encyclopedia of Local History* (2000; 2nd ed., Lanham, Md.: AltaMira Press, 2013), appendix B, pages 609–16. The Church of Jesus Christ of Latter-day Saints (LDS Church) has microfilmed and digitized many of the local records of other denominations, thereby simplifying and expediting access to these local religious records. A useful guide to writing a congregational or parish history is Laurence D. Fish, *Writing a Congregational History* (2003; rev. ed., Swarthmore, Penn.: National Episcopal Historians and Archivists, 2009).

BUSINESS RECORDS

The great tragedy of American business history is that most businesses have destroyed their records. A few major corporations such as the Ford Motor Company, Eli Lilly and Company, and the DuPont Company have developed well-organized corporate archives. A useful guide is the Directory of Corporate Archives in the United States and Canada, Society of

American Archivists (www2.archivists.org/groups/business-archives-section/directory-of-corporate-archives-in-the-united-states-and-canada-introduction). Some smaller businesses have donated their historical records to state and local historical societies. But most businesses have destroyed their records. In the twenty-first century, a driving force behind the destruction of business records has been the desire to avoid legal liability. During the notorious ENRON scandal in 2001, Nancy Temple, a lawyer with Arthur Andersen (the accounting firm representing ENRON), e-mailed Michael Odom, an Andersen partner in Houston, Texas, reminding him of the Andersen document retention and destruction policy. He forwarded the e-mail to a coworker with the now-infamous suggestion that "it might be useful to consider reminding the engagement team of our documentation and retention policy."[10] As a result of such euphemisms and the desire to maintain plausible deniability, many of the source materials for business history have been lost. Corporations (for-profit as well as nonprofit) must file annual reports—which can be fertile sources for business history—with the secretary of state in the state where they are incorporated. For a database of corporate annual reports since 1884, see ProQuest Historical Annual Reports (www.proquest.com/en-US/catalogs/databases/detail/pq_hist_annual_repts.shtml; subscription required). A useful introduction to the field of business history is K. Austin Kerr, Amos J. Loveday, and Mansel G. Blackford, *Local Businesses: Exploring Their History* (Nearby History Series; Nashville, Tenn.: American Association for State and Local History, 1990).

MILITARY RECORDS

The local, state, federal, and independent libraries and archives described above all have military records in their collections. Those range from personal records (diaries and correspondence) of serving personnel (enlisted, noncommissioned officers, and commissioned officers) to government records on the colonial, state, and federal levels documenting the armed conflicts from the colonial era to the present. Voluminous record groups in the National Archives document each of the military services during war and peace. State records provide evidence of militia and National Guard units' service in the armed conflicts in which they served. Military pension applications in both federal and state archives provide evidence of the military service of individual personnel. Unit diaries and after-action reports document the movements and battles of those units. Museums and monument commissions on the state and federal level preserve artifacts such as the Civil War regimental banners.

TRAVEL ACCOUNTS

Travel accounts written by outsiders provide insightful perspectives for local history. The Jesuit *Relations* (1632–1673) and other missionary records, Philip Vickers Fithian (1775–1776), Charles Maurice de Talley-rand-Périgord (1794–1796), Alexis de Tocqueville (1831–1832), Frances Trollope (1832), Harriet Martineau (1834), Charles Dickens (1842), Robert Louis Stevenson (1883), and Ian Fleming (1963) contributed accounts to the growing body of travel literature on the United States and Canada. Local reaction to George Washington's Southern Tour (1791), James Monroe's two Goodwill Tours (1817), Harry Truman's Whistle-Stop Campaign (1948), and other political campaigns highlight the linkage between local and national history. Some authors not only commented on but also contributed to the social and political movements that they described. Hinton Rowan Helper's *The Impending Crisis in the South: How to Meet It* (1857) provided a geopolitical analysis and itself became a catalyst in the events leading to the Civil War. Visits by prominent outsiders—such as the Marquis de Lafayette (1824–1825); Prince Maximilian of Wied-Neuwied (1832–1834); the Prince of Wales, later King Edward VII (1860); Winston Churchill (who visited the United States and Canada fifteen times between 1895 and 1961); and King George VI and Queen Elizabeth (1939)—provide a connection between local and international history. Also be alert to reportage by "internal tourists" such as Theodore Roosevelt (1888), Mark Twain (notably *Roughing It* [1872], *Old Times on the Mississippi* [1876], and *Life on the Mississippi* [1883]), Henry James (1907), and Theodore Dreiser (1916). The comments of such visitors, flattering or unflattering, welcome or unwelcome, can be a telescope (for the big picture) or a microscope (for the minutiae) focusing on the local community.

MAPS, ATLASES, GAZETTEERS, AND GEOGRAPHIC NAME AUTHORITIES

Maps provide a snapshot of geographical knowledge at the time of their creation. No more or less than any other primary source, maps convey the assumptions of their creators (often the victors in military, social, and economic contests). Among the factors to look for in maps is geopolitics—the politics of geography. The local, state, federal, and independent libraries described above have collections of maps and atlases (notably the Newberry Library [www.newberry.org] in Chicago and its Hermon Dunlap Smith Center for the History of Cartography). The last quarter of the nineteenth century witnessed an outpouring of not only county histories but also county maps, gazetteers, and atlases. David E. Kyvig and Myron A. Marty's *Nearby History: Exploring the Past around You* (1982; 3rd ed., Lanham, Md.: AltaMira Press, 2010), pages 78–85, provides insightful guidance on how to use maps as historical evidence. The Getty Thesaurus of Geographic Names Online (www.getty.edu/research/tools/vocabulary/tgn) is a structured vocabulary, including names and descriptions of places important for art and architecture. The U.S. Board of Geographic Names (BGN), an agency of the U.S. Geological Survey, was founded in 1890 to maintain uniform geographic name usage throughout the federal government. A researcher can search for geographic names on its website (http://geonames.usgs.gov).

EVIDENCE: WHERE DO YOU FIND IT?
(DOCUMENTARY EDITIONS)

Editions of primary documents loom large both in the research for and as an important part of local history publications. As you conduct the research on your local history subject, be alert for published documentary editions, which are more accessible and easier to use than archival manuscripts. Documentary editions provide transcriptions of manuscript materials and are available in print in the holdings of major university and public libraries and online.

The National Historical Publications and Records Commission (an agency of the National Archives and Records Administration) endorses editions that meet professional standards. For a list of such editions, see *Historical Documentary Editions: A Descriptive List of Documentary Publications Supported or Endorsed by the National Historical Publications and Records Commission* (Washington, D.C.: National Archives and Records Administration, 2000), www.archives.gov/nhprc/projects/publishing/catalog.pdf. All such editions, whether focusing on the papers of an individual person or on a topic of national importance, are relevant to local history and can be accessed through their tables of contents and their item-level indexes.

Documentary editions have formed a major part of the publications of state and local historical societies from their inception two centuries ago. They constitute the seed corn or the fundamental building blocks of history writing in its local and all other subject areas. Documentary editions are crucial to the research enterprise. But because their sales potential is minimal, they are appropriate for online publication in the twenty-first century. Even volumes in the print editions of founding fathers projects sell only about seven hundred copies. Their viability depends on publication subventions from the National Historical Publications and Records Commission. Many of the major documentary editions are now available simultaneously in print and online at sites such as the University of Virginia Press's Rotunda Project (http://rotunda.upress.virginia.edu), which was created for the publication of original digital scholarship along with newly digitized critical and documentary editions in the humanities and social sciences. The Rotunda Project makes accessible digital editions of the papers of, among others, George Washington, Alexander Hamilton, Thomas Jefferson, James Madison, Dolley Madison, Eliza Lucas Pinckney and Harriott Pinckney Horry, the Adams Papers, and the Documentary History of the Ratification of the Constitution. Documentary editions on local as well as national topics are now often published in simultaneous print and digital formats. Some are "born digital" and available online only.

Modern American documentary editing began with Clarence Edwin Carter's *The Territorial Papers of the United States*, 26 vols. (Washington, D.C.: Government Printing Office, 1934–1962). Carter was a professor of history at Miami University in Ohio. From 1931 the project was housed at the State Department, which has jurisdiction over the federal territories, and from 1950 at the National Archives. Modern documentary editing came into its own with the post–World War II editions of the papers of the founding fathers. These modern editions were comprehensive and collected. Comprehensive editions make accessible the papers—correspondence to and from, and other documents such as speeches, essays, and reports—of a prominent person, the subject of the edition. Some editions are organized around a particular historical topic such as the ratification of the Constitution or emancipation. Collected editions bring together the texts of original documents currently housed in collections in disparate repositories (libraries and archives) throughout the world. Many documentary editions include annotation that identifies persons and places and provides background and context for the user.

If you are planning a publication that may include both documentary and narrative elements, you will need to decide whether your publication will be a narrative history or a documentary edition. You should not consider a Victorian-style life-and-letters, which will fulfill nether function well. If you have a number of edited documents that could enhance the narrative text, you could add these verbatim as appendixes at the end of your publication. When preparing a documentary edition for publication, you should transcribe the document using the original spelling, punctuation, and capitalization. Such literal transcription is the modern standard, is the easiest to describe (you must describe your transcription method in an editorial method statement at the beginning of your edition), and is usually no impediment to a modern reader.

Standard introductions to the subject include Mary-Jo Kline and Susan Holbrook Perdue, *A Guide to Documentary Editing* (1987; 3rd ed., Charlottesville: University of Virginia Press, 2008); Michael E. Stevens and Steven B. Burg, *Editing Historical Documents: A Handbook of Practice* (Lanham, Md.: AltaMira Press, 1997); and Beth E. Luey, ed., *Editing Documents and Texts: An Annotated Bibliography* (Madison, Wisc.: Madison House, 1990).

ILLUSTRATION RESEARCH

Well-chosen illustrations enhance a publication. They supplement and amplify the text and provide the author with a medium, in addition to the text, to communicate and engage with the reader. An author can also increase the likelihood that an editor will favorably consider an article or book for publication if the author has identified potential illustrations. Many of the categories of repositories listed above under the section "Primary Sources for Local History"—state and local libraries, archives, museums, and historical societies—have visual collections (prints, photographs, postcards, paintings, sculpture, and artifacts) and finding aids to facilitate research in those collections. David E. Kyvig and Myron A. Marty's *Nearby History: Exploring the Past around You* (1982; 3rd ed., Lanham, Md.: AltaMira Press, 2010), pages 133–48, helpfully explains how to analyze photographs as historical evidence. Local newspapers often maintain photographic archives; some have transferred their historic photographs to a local library or historical society. Stock photography is a large potential source for the licensing of historic images. The largest stock photography agencies are Getty Images (www.gettyimages.com) and Corbis (www.corbisimages.com).

PastPerfect-Online (http://pastperfect-online.com) is a database of artifact collections at more than 300 museums, libraries, and archives, containing more than 2.7 million records. The researcher can locate images and information using Artifact Search or browse through the collections, filtering by region or specialty to narrow the list.

Several federal agencies have collections that are relevant to local history, including:

- The Library of Congress's Prints and Photographs Division (www. loc.gov/rr/print) has a collection of more than fourteen million images with an online catalog, collection guides and finding aids, and guidelines for obtaining reproductions and permission to publish.
- The National Archives' Still Picture Branch (www.archives.gov/research/guides/still-pictures-guide.html) maintains a collection of approximately six million photographs and graphics with an online collection guide and an archival research catalog.
- The National Portrait Gallery has a collection of twenty-one thousand works of art (paintings, sculpture, prints, drawings, and photographs) focusing on images of famous and not-so-famous Americans from all regions of the country. See *National Portrait Gallery, Smithsonian Institution: Permanent Collection Illustrated Checklist*, Dru Dowdy, comp., photographs by Eugene Mantie and Rolland G. White (1973; 25th Anniversary ed., Washington, D.C.: Published by the National Portrait Gallery in association with the Smithsonian Institution Press, 1987). The researcher can search the

National Portrait Gallery's collection at http://npgportraits.si.edu/
emuseumnpg/code/emuseum.asp?page=search_basicNPG&
module=NPG&profile=NPG. The National Portrait Gallery's Portal
to American Portraits (http://npgportraits.si.edu/emuseumCAP/
code/emuseum.asp) is a database that provides access to more than
one hundred thousand records from the Catalog of American Portraits (CAP), a survey of American portraits in public and private
collections across the United States and other countries.

The rules of copyright and acknowledging authorship of written
records (manuscript or print, published or unpublished) also apply to
visual materials such as prints, photographs, paintings, and sculpture. If
the author has commissioned such a visual work, if the creator is alive, or
if the work is otherwise protected by copyright (see the discussion of
copyright in chapter 3), then the author will need to obtain permission to
publish the work from the copyright owner and probably pay a usage fee
(see also appendix 4: "Sample Contract with a Photographer"). Even if
the work itself is in the public domain, if it is in the collection of an
institution (such as a library, archive, museum, or historical society), the
author/user will need to obtain a publication-quality print or digital file
of a photograph of the work and permission to publish it (and pay required fees) from the institution that owns the work. The University of
Chicago Press has an excellent discussion of art permissions and downloadable permission request templates (for text and art, copyright, and
use) at www.press.uchicago.edu/infoServices/permissions.html.

Captions should concisely describe an illustration and not repeat information already covered in the text of a publication. A caption description should include the name of the creator (photographer or artist) of the
work in the illustration, the name of the institution that owns the work,
and the name of the collection of which the work is a part. By providing
such caption information, an author not only complies with legal requirements and professional courtesy but also provides background and con-
textual information on the illustration that will be useful to the reader.
Beware of errors in captions, which are sometimes written by persons
other than the author of the text of a publication. Also beware of flopped
(left to right) images, a common error in publishing illustrations.

THE TRANSITION FROM RESEARCH TO WRITING

The research and writing phases of a publication project (be it of article or
book length) will overlap. An essential first step in planning a project is to
develop a précis that will include a chapter outline of the entire project.
The chapter outline will then be your guide through both the research
and the writing phases of your project. The chapter outline will help to
give you a sense of where you are going, where you have come from, and

what remains to be done on the project. As you conduct your research, you will inevitably find that you have reached a critical mass or a point of diminishing returns, beyond which you should start writing. As the next chapter (on writing) will make clear, the process of writing will expose to the author the gaps and loose ends in the research that may require a return to the sources. So the earlier you get started writing on the basis of your research, the better!

NOTES

1. For guidelines on how to analyze artifacts as historical evidence, see E. McClung Fleming, "Artifact Study: A Proposed Model," in *Material Culture Studies in America,* ed. Thomas J. Schlereth (Nashville, Tenn.: American Association for State and Local History, 1982), 162–73; Cary Carson, "Doing History with Material Culture," in *Material Culture and the Study of American Life,* ed. M. G. Quimby (New York: W. W. Norton, 1978), 41–64; Jules David Prown, "Mind in Matter: An Introduction to Material Culture Theory and Method," *Winterthur Portfolio* 17 (1982): 17–37; David E. Kyvig and Myron A. Marty, *Nearby History: Exploring the Past around You* (1982; 3rd ed., Lanham, Md.: AltaMira Press, 2010), 159–75; and *The Oxford Handbook of Material Culture Studies,* ed. Dan Hicks and Mary C. Beaudry (New York: Oxford University Press, 2010).

2. IHR.org, "About," n.d., www.ihr.org/about.

3. "Mission and History (American Memory from the Library of Congress)," n.d., http://memory.loc.gov/ammem/about/index.html.

4. Christine A. Pruzin, "State Digital Resources (Virtual Programs & Services, Library of Congress)," n.d., www.loc.gov/rr/program/bib/statememory. Another valuable resource is Dennis A. Trinkle and Scott A. Merriman, eds., *The American History Highway: A Guide to Internet Resources in U.S., Canadian, and Latin American History* (Armonk, N.Y.: M. E. Sharpe, 2007), which provides extensive annotated lists of historically related websites.

5. Albert N. Greco, Clara E. Rodríguez, and Robert M. Wharton, *The Culture and Commerce of Publishing in the 21st Century* (Stanford, Calif.: Stanford Business Books, 2007), 76.

6. Virginia Cole, "Local History Resources Online," in *Encyclopedia of Local History,* ed. Carol Kammen and Amy H. Wilson (2000; 2nd ed., Lanham, Md.: AltaMira Press, 2013), 323–35. For a useful analysis of the strengths and weaknesses of online source materials, see Jeffrey G. Barlow, "Historical Research and Electronic Evidence: Problems and Promises," in *Writing, Teaching, and Researching History in the Electronic Age: Historians and Computers,* ed. Dennis A. Trinkle (Armonk, N.Y.: M. E. Sharpe, 1998), 194–225.

7. "DOAJ—Directory of Open Access Journals," www.doaj.org.

8. Jeff Howe, Crowdsourcing Blog, "Crowdsourcing: A Definition," June 2, 2006, http://crowdsourcing.typepad.com/cs/2006/06/crowdsourcing_a.html (accessed January 6, 2013).

9. Lori Byrd Phillips and Dominic McDevitt-Parks, "Historians in *Wikipedia*: Building an Open, Collaborative History," *Perspectives in History: The Newsmagazine of the American Historical Association* 50, no. 9 (December 2012): 55–56.

10. "Andersen's Share of Enron Scandal Grows," CNN Money, January 15, 2003, http://money.cnn.com/2002/01/15/news/andersen/index.htm (accessed July 18, 2011).

THREE

Communication: How Do You Shape a Specialized Subject for a Nonspecialist Audience? (Writing)

Research and writing *con*verge on the specialized topic but *di*verge to provide context and background sufficient to make that topic intelligible to a nonspecialist audience. Research and writing are not clearly compartmentalized phases; they inform and reinforce each other. Writing will reveal gaps and loose ends that will require a return to research. Research is not conducted randomly or in a vacuum; the researcher needs a précis that will include a chapter outline and a concept of the finished product in order to give direction to the research. The researcher needs to have some idea of where the research is going. But research often leads to unexpected surprises (pleasant and otherwise).

John Ruston Pagan, an early American legal historian at the University of Richmond School of Law, recounted in *Anne Orthwood's Bastard: Sex and Law in Early Virginia* (New York: Oxford University Press, 2003) the long-term consequences of a seventeenth-century affair between Anne Orthwood, an indentured servant, and John Kendall, the privileged protégé of a colonial gentry family. In his study, which won the American Historical Association's Prize in Atlantic History, Pagan explains the opportunity that a rich and long-running archival record presents to the local historian:

> For the case-study technique to work, the author must be able to sketch fairly detailed portraits of the characters in the drama, depicting their family backgrounds, their socioeconomic status, their relationships with other characters, and various factors influencing their conduct. Such a portrayal is possible for the Orthwood-Kendall litigation because of the richness of the Eastern Shore archives. Northampton and

its northern neighbor, Accomack County, possess the oldest continuous series of county court records in the United States. Unlike the records of most Virginia counties and the archives of the colony's central court, the judicial manuscripts of the Eastern Shore survived the ravages of the American Revolution and the Civil War. They begin with an entry for January 7, 1633, and proceed, in a virtually unbroken sequence, to the present day. These documents, augmented by English sources such as parish registers and lists of indentured servants, permit us to reconstruct the story of Anne Orthwood's bastard.[1]

With those records to draw on, Pagan wove an intricate and extended narrative of the affair and its consequences:

> John Kendall and Anne Orthwood brought misery to their lives when they surrendered to their passions on that weekend so long ago. Their affair produced embarrassment for him and death for her. For us, however, the well-documented consequences of their misadventure yield much that is valuable. John and Anne's story helps us appreciate the adaptability of English law and understand the process by which Virginians created their own legal identity just two generations after the first settlers landed.[2]

The gentry community's legal authority—the Northampton County Court—closed ranks and in 1664 found John Kendall financially liable and responsible for the paternity of Jasper Orthwood (Anne's son) but declared him morally innocent, thus preserving his social standing and reputation in the community. But Pagan recounts an unexpected turn of events and the reversal of John Kendall's fortunes:

> At this point, John undoubtedly thought he had put the Orthwood scandal behind him. He had fulfilled his financial responsibilities, found Jasper a master, and done everything he could to clear his name. He did not reckon, however, on the maverick natures of the twelve men who made up the Northampton County grand jury. On February 23, 1665, the jurors embarrassed the Kendalls anew by charging John with the crime of fornication. The justices, who just six months earlier had declared John blameless, found themselves in the awkward position of having to direct the sheriff to summon him for trial.[3]

Nathaniel Philbrick, director of the Egan Institute of Maritime Studies on Nantucket Island and a research fellow at the Nantucket Historical Association, wove an arresting narrative of a nineteenth-century whaling voyage in his *In the Heart of the Sea: The Tragedy of the Whaleship* Essex (New York: Viking, 2000). The winner of the National Book Award for Nonfiction, Philbrick's book recounted the appalling discovery by the crew of a Nantucket whaleship, the *Dauphin*, as it cruised off the Chilean coast in 1821. The ship's captain, Zimri Coffin, trained his telescope on a drifting whaleboat:

Under Coffin's watchful eye, the helmsman brought the ship as close as possible to the derelict craft. Even though their momentum quickly swept them past it, the brief seconds during which the ship loomed over the open boat presented a sight that would stay with the crew the rest of their lives.

First they saw bones—human bones—littering the thwarts and floorboards, as if the whaleboat were the seagoing lair of a ferocious, man-eating beast. Then they saw the two men. They were curled up in opposite ends of the boat, their skin covered with sores, their eyes bulging from the hollows of their skulls, their beards caked with salt and blood. They were sucking the marrow from the bones of their dead shipmates.

Instead of greeting their rescuers with smiles of relief, the survivors—too delirious with thirst and hunger to speak—were disturbed, even frightened. They jealously clutched the splintered and gnawed-over bones with a desperate, almost feral intensity, refusing to give them up, like two starving dogs found trapped in a pit.

Later, once the survivors had been given some food and water (and had finally surrendered the bones), one of them found the strength to tell his story. It was a tale made of a whaleman's worst nightmares: of being in a boat far from land with nothing left to eat or drink and—perhaps worst of all—of a whale with the vindictiveness and guile of a man.[4]

A writer of history (whether academic or popular) has an ethical obligation to seek the whole truth. In pursuit of the whole truth, a writer of history needs certain core competencies. Notable among those core competencies is the ability to assess evidence and to ascertain cause and effect. A writer of history must also be free to pursue and publish the results of research wherever the evidence may lead.

Embarked on research for a biography of Ralph Lauren, Michael Gross described how his project began as an authorized biography with the subject's full cooperation. But as the author got into the project, the subject became more controlling and concerned about the public relations/corporate identity ramifications of the project. Ultimately author and subject parted ways, and Gross wrote his own book. Examples like that are legion.

In January 2000, my publisher agreed to a Lauren book, and I called [Hamilton] South [then the president of Polo Ralph Lauren] to discuss it in more detail. Halfway through the conversation, he asked, "What about Ralph's private life?" I told him biographies were about lives. I would want to write about Ralph's business life and personal life, and about the places where they mingled. South started to hem and haw, and I realized what the problem was. . . . Then I got out of there as fast as I could and called my agent and my editor. "Maybe you'll be better off without him," my editor said.[5]

History at its core and at its best is a study of cause and effect. During the ancient and medieval periods, the best historians—those still read today—rose above mere chronicle and provided explanations for the course of events. A chronicle is a historical account of events arranged in order of time, often devoid of analysis or interpretation. Or as they say in the Marine Corps, "Two hundred years of tradition, unhampered by progress." Ancient and modern times have their chronicles and lists of rulers, events, dates, and ancestral lines. An occupational hazard of history writing is antiquarianism—the compilation of minute data with little or no analysis, explanation, or narrative. If you seek to engage an audience, in whatever medium, you must provide that analysis, explanation, and narrative. More than half a century ago, Christopher Coleman observed, "Waste of effort on nonessentials is easily prevented by keeping before one the question: What would an intelligent outsider want to know about this community, or about this subject? . . . The goal of all historical effort," noted Coleman, is "the understanding of the world in which we live."[6]

PRESCRIPTIONS FOR GOOD WRITING

Prescriptions for good writing abound, and aspiring authors will make themselves familiar with the best of them. The preeminent twentieth-century English essayist, George Orwell, concisely declared six rules for writers in his "Politics and the English Language," first published in the journal *Horizon* (1946):

- Never use a metaphor, simile, or other figure of speech which you are used to seeing in print.
- Never use a long word where a short one will do.
- If it is possible to cut a word out, always cut it out.
- Never use the passive voice where you can use the active.
- Never use a foreign phrase, a scientific word, or a jargon word if you can think of an everyday English equivalent.
- Break any of these rules sooner than say anything outright barbarous.

Teachers who have read quantities of student writing will detect variations on Orwell's appeal for simplicity in language:
Inexperienced writers:

- use large and obscure words
- use impersonal ("it was" or "there were") constructions
- rely (with brain unengaged) on spell check, which will not alert the user when he or she is using a real word that is the wrong word in the context

Experienced writers:

- use common words in uncommon ways
- use personal constructions and strong verbs
- follow Mark Twain's advice: "As to the adjective: when in doubt, cut it out."[7]
- know that brevity and conciseness are harder—but more desirable—to achieve than verbosity and vagueness
- proofread their writing
- quote sparingly, reserving verbatim quotations to the most telling and illustrative examples
- revise and rewrite, understanding that more than one draft will be a necessary and normal part of the analytical and writing process

One of the most valuable guides to basic writing skills is William Strunk Jr. and E. B. White, *The Elements of Style* (1918; 4th ed., New York: Longman: 1999). Strunk, the sole author of the first edition of this book, taught English at Cornell University. One of his students, E. B. White (author of books ostensibly for children such as *Charlotte's Web* and *Stuart Little*), revised the book, and it has deservedly become a classic. Widely known simply as Strunk & White, this style guide is available in many forms, both print and online, including a 2005 edition that is illustrated. While some of its admonitions may strike modern ears as out of date, most still have value, especially for editors of a certain vintage for whom the improper use of "less" and "fewer" or "literally" can be tantamount to a declaration of illiteracy.

THE STYLE CONVENTIONS

Two major style conventions—for the presentation of punctuation, abbreviations, and source citations—are available in the field of history. The nature of your audience will determine which style convention you should use. If your article or book will be published by a full-service publisher that provides a copy editor, ask your publisher what style convention to use. If you hope to engage a popular, mass audience, the *Associated Press Stylebook and Briefing on Media Law*, edited by Daniel Christian, Sally Jacobsen, and David Minthorn (1953; rev. new ed., New York: Associated Press, 2012) will be appropriate. Used by broadcast and print journalists, the latest edition of the *Associated Press Stylebook* has expanded chapters on social media and broadcasting, including online video.

If you intend to reach a specialist, scholarly audience, you will want to use *The Chicago Manual of Style* (1906; 16th ed., Chicago: University of Chicago Press, 2010). Serious authors will need to become thoroughly familiar with *The Chicago Manual*. Authors and editors refer to it for questions and answers concerning style (see especially part 2: "Style and Usage," and part 3: "Documentation," especially chapter 14: "Documentation I: Notes and Bibliography"). Both first time and experienced authors can benefit from examining part 1: "The Publishing Process," chapter 1: "Books and Journals" ("The Parts of a Book," "The Parts of a Journal," and "Considerations for Web-Based Publications"). Authors of all levels of experience or none need to be thoroughly familiar with chapter 2: "Manuscript Preparation, Manuscript Editing, and Proofreading"; chapter 16: "Indexes"; and appendix A: "Production and Digital Technology."

PRELIMINARY MANUSCRIPT PREPARATION

Before contacting a publisher, an author needs to conduct some due diligence. An author needs to find out if a publisher responds to e-mail (as opposed to surface mail), requires the use of certain word processing programs, or wants to see a full manuscript or a proposal. An author needs to examine the publisher's guidelines for authors, which all publishers have. Keep in mind, during preliminary manuscript preparation, that an author should not submit to a prospective publisher a manuscript that looks like a book—that is, margins should be unjustified, end-of-line words should be unhyphenated, and type should not appear in bold. On all these matters, consult the publisher's guidelines for authors.

Authors will find especially helpful the discussion of preliminary manuscript preparation in Robert Lee Brewer, ed., *Writer's Market* (1922; 92nd ed., Cincinnati: Writer's Digest Books, 2012). This is an annual publication. In the 1931 edition, H. L. Mencken as editor of the *American Mercury* famously explained his criteria for publishing articles. Particularly useful for first time authors are the sections on "Finding Work" (and within it, "Query Letter Clinic" and "Publishers and Their Imprints"), "Managing Work" (and within it, the chapters on contracts and "Time Management and Organization for Writers"), "Promoting Work," "Markets" (and within it, "Book Publishers"). The latter section is highly serviceable for contact information and subject areas on which publishers seek manuscripts. See also the section on "Consumer Magazines" (especially the part on "History"). Another helpful title from the same publisher is Wendy Burt-Thomas, *The Writer's Digest Guide to Query Letters* (Cincinnati: Writer's Digest Books, 2009). Another useful annual directory with contact information and subject areas on which publishers seek manuscripts is Karen Hallard, Mary-Anne Lutter, and Vivian Sposobiec, *Literary Market Place: The Directory of the American Book Publishing Industry with Industry Yellow Pages*, 2 vols. (1940; 70th ed., Medford, N.J.: Information Today, 2011).

Experience is the best teacher of writing. A previously unpublished author should gain experience writing and getting article-length studies published on local history. The discipline of seeking publication outlets, soliciting publishers, dealing with and responding to editors, and receiving critiques and feedback from knowledgeable colleagues in the field, will provide valuable lessons. Through such experience, a writer of local history will learn what has already been done and who is currently doing what in the subject field. Writing and publishing are integral parts of networking in the field—processes by which you can get to know and become known by colleagues in the field. Newspapers, magazines, and newsletters of local historical organizations can provide outlets for book reviews, columns, and features on local history topics. Also, peer-reviewed state historical journals can provide opportunities for local history writers engaged in substantive research. The website of the Brown University Library offers an excellent list of state historical journals with links to corresponding websites.[8] The experience gained in writing and getting article-length studies published will serve a writer well before tackling the large-scale task of organizing and writing a book.

Regardless of whether one is writing an article or a manuscript to submit for book publication, successful authors carefully study the information provided by the prospective publishers for their benefit. They are familiar with each specific publisher's list or, in the case of a journal, the kind of articles that have appeared in the journal over the past year at least. Nothing is more irritating to an editor than receiving a call or query from authors who are obviously not familiar with the previous work the publisher has done, or who do not show knowledge of significant work already done in the field in which they are working. While it is the job of editors to find suitable material for publication and while the best of them are open and curious, they can nevertheless quickly shut down when they realize for any number of reasons that an author's work is not in their ballpark. The author's job is to keep the editor and the reader interested, and that is done through the quality of the writing one submits. Good writing can often trump familiarity with a publisher's work, but most often poor writing and lack of attention to author's guidelines go hand in hand.

In his chapter "Writing," Thomas Felt asked his readers to consider the writing they have done in their lives, including letters of all kinds, articles, and school assignments, and to think about when that writing was most effective. He asserted that any effective communication is the result of some kind of feeling or emotion that "fuels the curiosity" of an author. "It matters little what the emotion is—affection, amusement, awe, indignation, or even disgust," he wrote. "The stimulus is what counts. Nothing good has ever been written out of boredom."

While such passion is a necessary condition for effective communication, it is not a sufficient one. Writing ability is also the result of a lifelong "involvement in the craftsmanship of writing," and a dedication to mastering the conventions and expectations of the craft. As with any craft, one does not acquire mastery overnight. Improvement is a gradual process that is the result of one's own experience, as mentioned above, and also learning from the work of others. Felt identified a couple of ways that a writer can learn from the experience of others, which we will explore here: models and conventions.[9]

Models are simply examples of good writing that one can seek to emulate. To do so involves analysis of what makes the model writing effective. When the authors of this book were editing the Indiana Historical Society's magazine *Traces of Indiana and Midwestern History*, we encouraged prospective authors, especially in the early years, to look at examples of successful articles that had been previously published in the magazine and, regardless of the topic, try to match them in terms of language, length, structure, style, use of illustrations, and documentation. We were looking for a melding of journalistic style and historical accuracy that would appeal to a broad audience of intelligent readers. We were not asking scholars to "dumb down" their work; we were asking them instead to present their research in a way that would be accessible to a general audience. Conversely, we encouraged journalists to use sources beyond telephone interviews, to write paragraphs that were longer than one or two sentences, and to follow the style conventions for scholarly publishing (*Chicago Manual of Style*) rather than those of newspaper journalism (*Associated Press Stylebook*). All authors were asked to tell a story scrupulously based on evidence that would engage a reader.

To celebrate the tenth anniversary of the launching of the quarterly illustrated magazine *Traces of Indiana and Midwestern History*, the editors asked authors who had contributed articles during the magazine's first ten years to choose a visual image (for example, a painting, print, or photograph) that they considered historically revealing and briefly analyze it. George Geib, professor of history at Butler University, compared the old Marion County Courthouse and the new City-County Building that replaced it. The old and the new structures briefly stood adjacent to each other before the old courthouse was demolished.

> Separated by forty feet, ninety years, and a conceptual revolution in architecture and design, two Marion County courthouses stand back to front in this 1961 Bass photograph.
>
> In the foreground is the county's contribution to the 1876 centennial year. Exuberant and eclectic, it is a study in the elaboration of the Second Empire style. Renaissance orders parade around its window lines, while modern cast-iron railings and balconies compete with statuary and triumphant stairways for our attention. Built in an era of intense political competition, it is a palace of popular sovereignty.
>
> In the background is the city and county's joint contribution to the modern resurgence of downtown Indianapolis. Solidly vertical and starkly functional, it is a series of glass and stone facades that affirms the best and the worst in modernism. Built in an era of bureaucracy

Figure 3.1. **The Marion County Courthouse (1876), designed by Isaac M. Hodgson, stands briefly cheek by jowl in Indianapolis next to the City-County Building (1962), designed by Wright, Porteous and Associates. (*Photograph by Bass Photo Company, Indiana Historical Society, IHS 307517-1.*)**

and efficiency, it is a corporate headquarters placed at the service of government. . . .

The most important cause of this dramatic architectural face-off was probably the alarm felt by many Indianapolis boosters in the 1950s, concerned they were lagging behind other Midwestern cities in creating a promotional high-rise skyline. Whether as an incentive to further downtown investment, as a rebuttal to growing suburbanization, or as a means of laying the lingering ghosts of the Great Depression to rest, the lure of downtown revitalization was catching the imagination of a new generation of local leaders. The City-County Building was one of government's contributions to that new city, surely incorporating the hope that it would soon be dwarfed by other new structures supported by increased private resources.

Forty years ago, there was no room for the old alongside the new on the courthouse block. The 1876 structure was scheduled to remain only long enough for the move to the new structure to be completed. But far from winning universal acclaim that another old building was going, the ensuing demolition became one of the defining events in the emergence of the current historic preservation movement in Indianapolis. Just as the wrecker's ball was about to strike, a court injunction delayed the process to permit alternatives to be sought. . . .

All who have been touched by the modern historic preservation movement have seen comparable scenes somewhere in their communities as tradition and development clash over private or public space. Today we are often assured that preservationist and developer are natural partners, with far more interests in common than in conflict. But this photo captures a moment when those two concerns stared at one another across a narrow space too deep to admit compromise, giving visual expression to the stark choices that admirers of Hoosier history sometimes confront as they strive to affirm both the present and the past.[10]

As we developed the magazine, we developed a style of writing and a group of writers on both sides of the scholarship/journalism divide who understood what we were doing and became adept at producing pieces for *Traces*. Because many publishers of books and journals on local history are also looking for this ideal synthesis of journalism and scholarship, it is worth describing in some detail.

Most important, it involves the ability to recognize and marshal the different modes of writing—narration, description, and exposition—in presenting well-researched information that is interesting to read. Historical narrative involves relaying a sequence of events, usually in the order in which they happened. Good narrative history appears to be easy to write because it is easy to read, but like pleasing music that is easy to listen to, it is the result of a good deal of experience, training, and talent. A blues musician once explained that the most important notes in a guitar solo were the ones he did not play. Likewise, the key to telling an interesting story is knowing what to include and what to leave out.

In *A Short Guide to Writing about History*, Richard Marius and Melvin E. Page write, "A good narrative begins by establishing some sort of tension, some kind of problem that later development of the narration should resolve." Narrative also has a climax that comes near the end, ties up all its strands, and "embodies the meaning the writer wants readers to take from the story."[11] All who watch movies or read novels are familiar with this narrative arc, but presenting history as narrative, with dialogue, action, suspense, and resolution involves special skills because the historian cannot embellish for the sake of enhancing the drama but must adhere to what is known and can be proved.

EXEMPLARS OF EFFECTIVE HISTORICAL WRITING

There are many historians whose work offers especially good models for narrative history, and they have been rewarded with large audiences of readers and many awards. Barbara W. Tuchman, who won Pulitzer Prizes for *The Guns of August* (1962) and *Stilwell and the American Experience in China, 1911–45* (1971) and who is well known for many other bestselling works of history, offers particularly good models for aspiring historians. She began her career as a journalist—as an editorial assistant for *The Nation* (at that time owned by her father) and as an American correspondent for the *New Statesman* in London. During World War II she worked as an editor for the United States Office of War Information. "The writer's object is—or should be—to hold the reader's attention," she once said. "I want the reader to turn the page and keep on turning to the end." She added, "This is accomplished only when the narrative moves steadily ahead, not when it comes to a weary standstill, overloaded with every item uncovered in the research." [12]

David McCullough, another Pulitzer Prize–winning author for both his *Truman* (1992) and *John Adams* (2001), provides excellent models for emulation as well. Like Tuchman, he began his career as a magazine journalist. Experience working for *Sports Illustrated* and the popular history magazine *American Heritage* prepared McCullough to develop a popular style of history writing based on rigorous research.

In an interview with Bruce Cole, chairman of the National Endowment for the Humanities, McCullough cited some of the authors who provided the models he used to develop his style. These included Francis Parkman, Barbara Tuchman, Robert Caro, Shelby Foote, Bruce Catton, Paul Horgan, and Wallace Stegner. He also revealed much about his successful formula for writing history. Here is an excerpt from the interview:

> *Cole:* It seems to me that so much of history is about vast, impersonal forces which act on people. Your books are not about that. Your books are about people, their strengths, their flaws, their heroism. I think that's one of the reasons that people are so drawn to your books.
>
> *McCullough:* Well, Barbara Tuchman said, "There's no trick to interesting people in history or children in history." She said, "You can explain it in two words: Tell stories." . . .
>
> First of all, you can make the argument that there's no such thing as the past. Nobody lived in the past. . . . They lived in the present. It is

their present, not our present, and they don't know how it's going to come out. They weren't just like we are because they lived in that very different time. You can't understand them if you don't understand how they perceived reality and you don't understand that unless you understand the culture. . . . What did they read? What poetry moved them? What music did they listen to? What did they eat? What were they afraid of? What was it like to travel from one place to another then? . . . That's one of the reasons I began *John Adams* as I did, with these two lone men on horseback riding through a bleak, cold winter landscape. For all intents and purposes, they're anonymous. They are coming through that winter scene, the snow and the wind, and they're going to ride nearly four hundred miles in that kind of weather, on horseback, to get to the Continental Congress in Philadelphia.[13]

And here is the beginning to *John Adams* that McCullough referred to above for consideration:

In the cold, nearly colorless light of a New England winter, two men on horseback traveled the coast road below Boston, heading north. A foot or more of snow covered the landscape, the remnants of a Christmas storm that had blanketed Massachusetts from one end of the province to the other. Beneath the snow, after weeks of severe cold, the ground was frozen solid to a depth of two feet. Packed ice in the road, ruts as hard as iron, made the going hazardous, and the riders, mindful of the horses, kept at a walk.

Nothing about the harsh landscape differed from other winters. Nor was there anything to distinguish the two riders, no signs of rank or title, no liveried retinue bringing up the rear. It might have been any year and they could have been anybody braving the weather for any number of reasons. Dressed as they were in heavy cloaks, their hats pulled low against the wind, they were barely distinguishable even from each other, except that the older, stouter of the two did most of the talking.

He was John Adams of Braintree and he loved to talk. He was a known talker. There were some, even among his admirers, who wished he talked less. He himself wished he talked less, and he had particular regard for those, like George Washington, who somehow managed great reserve under almost any circumstance.

John Adams was a lawyer and a farmer, a graduate of Harvard College, the husband of Abigail Smith Adams, the father of four children. He was forty years old and he was a revolutionary. . . .

As befitting a studious lawyer from Braintree, Adams was a "plain dressing" man. His oft-stated pleasures were his family, his farm, his books and writing table, a convivial pipe and cup of coffee (now that tea was no longer acceptable), or preferably a glass of good Madeira.

In the warm seasons he relished long walks and time alone on horseback. Such exercise, he believed, roused "the animal spirits" and "dispersed melancholy." He loved the open meadows of home, the "old acquaintances" of rock ledges and breezes from the sea. From his doorstep to the water's edge was approximately a mile.

He was a man who cared deeply for his friends, who, with few exceptions, were to be his friends for life, and in some instances despite severe strains. And to no one was he more devoted than to his wife, Abigail. She was his "Dearest Friend," as he addressed her in his letters—his "best, dearest, worthiest, wisest friend in the world"—while to her he was "the tenderest of husbands," her "good man." [14]

There is so much to commend and so much to learn from in this brief excerpt from a very long book that it is hard to know where to begin. While not a great deal is happening in a narrative sense, the reader perceives the narrative being established through a few of the tensions that will need to be resolved during the course of the story, not the least of which is whether or not these riders will even make it to their destination. The contrast between the verbose Adams and the reserved Washington and the difficulty of being away for long periods from Adams's beloved wife, family, and home will play out over the next seven hundred pages.

The passage is exemplary also in its execution of other modes of writing that are necessary tools of the historian's craft, such as description, exposition, and the use of quotations. Description is all about presenting sensory experience—what things look, feel, and taste like—in an effort to provide the reader with an understanding of what it was like to be with a particular person at a particular time and place. It is easy from McCullough's description to experience the cold and the darkness of the New England winter and the danger of the journey on which the riders have embarked. In just a few sentences, the reader also knows what John Adams looks like and something about his personality and even his character. Because sensory experiences can be similar across time periods, especially for local historians writing about a particular place that they know well, description can be a powerful tool to add vividness to historical writing and to capture the imagination of readers. Nevertheless, it must ring true and correspond with research. McCullough's descriptions do so, providing the reader with the necessary foundation for trusting that this story will be truthful. Flights of fancy not grounded in evidence can create a lack of trust on the part of the reader and cause embarrassment for the author.

Exposition is writing that explains and analyzes. In narrative writing it provides the background upon which the story is told. It is perhaps the most prevalent form of historical writing, consisting, as Marius and Page explain, of "philosophical ideas, causes of events, the significance of decisions, the motives of participants, the working of an organization, the ideology of a political party." [15] The best historical writing reflects a balance of narrative, description, and exposition, such as we see in McCullough's example. While we are feeling the winter chill and the uncertainty of the journey along with visualizing the protagonist's physical characteristics, we also learn that he dressed plainly, relished long walks, was prone to melancholy, loved his wife, and much more. Description properly administered can add interest to exposition, while exposition is necessary to provide meaning to the narrative.

Finally, McCullough's writing offers excellent examples of how to use quotations effectively in historical writing. Perhaps the most important thing to note in this regard is that the primary sources have been digested so thoroughly by the writer that they seem to appear almost effortlessly in support of the story. Drawn from writings done throughout Adams's life, they are offered in the beginning of the story as an introduction to his ways of thinking and writing and to his character. They reflect McCullough's mastery of the material, leaven the narrative with a personal touch in much the same way that quotations are used in journalistic writing, and provide the reader with trust by signaling that this story is based on exhaustive research in primary sources.

Studying models like Tuchman, McCullough, and many others who have developed the craft of writing history into an art is a fundamental key to becoming an effective writer of local history who is successfully published. Just as important, as Thomas Felt acknowledged, is an awareness and mastery of conventions, including various style manuals and generally accepted standards for good writing. It is not unknown for a busy editor to reject a proposal or a submission based simply on the recognition in the cover letter or the first few pages of a manuscript that the author has little understanding of certain basic conventions of the writing trade.

COPYRIGHT

Copyright is a large and complicated subject on which many books have been written and many courses taught. It is the means by which creators of original works are allowed to benefit from their creations. One of the best books for the purposes of a layperson who wants to understand the history, development, and intricacies of copyright, and be entertained as well is *The Illustrated Story of Copyright* by Edward Samuels, which deals not only with books but also includes issues and examples that cover the entire entertainment industry, including music, movies, and the Internet.[16] The website of the U.S. Copyright Office (www.copyright.gov) provides a great deal of information about copyright, including Copyright Law, Copyright Basics, Frequently Asked Questions, and various publications, reports, and studies that delve into the nuances and complexities of copyright protection. The site also allows searching copyright records from 1978 and access to online registration. Another useful introduction is Michael Les Benedict, *A Historian's Guide to Copyright* (Washington, D.C.: American Historical Association, 2012).

While it behooves authors of all kinds to understand the history and development of copyright law, the basic concerns of the author involve managing your own rights, as well as managing the rights of copyright holders whose material—literary or visual—may be included in your work. The first thing to know is that copyright protection now begins at the time the original work is created in a "fixed tangible form of expression." Registration is not required, but recommended in order to be eligible for compensation should infringement, or the unauthorized use of your work, occur. Copyright protection gives the owner the exclusive right to reproduce the work, create derivative works, distribute copies, and perform or display the work publicly. A copyright owner can transfer any or all of his or her exclusive rights, but the transfer must be done in writing and signed by the copyright owner. As mentioned in the next chapter, authors will likely want to consult with an attorney who specializes in intellectual property law when making decisions about managing rights in a publisher's contract.

The duration of copyright varies according to the date of a work's creation. A work created on or after January 1, 1979, is protected from its creation until seventy years after the death of the creator. Works created before 1923 are in the public domain and are copyright free, as are works published between 1923 and 1963 for which copyright registrations were not renewed. Works created between 1923 and 1963, however, may have been renewed and may still be protected. Works in this category must be considered individually. Unpublished works, such as manuscripts, letters, diaries, and photographs created before 1979, may also be problematic in terms of determining whether they are protected or in the public domain. Archivists and librarians can tell you whether or not their institutions have copyright to the materials in their collections. This would involve a written agreement of transfer signed by the copyright holder. Often, however, archival collections have not been formally transferred to the institutions in which they are held. In that case it is the author's responsibility to investigate the copyright status of materials he or she wishes to use. When using such materials, efforts to seek out copyright holders should be made and documented should unknown rights holders surface after publication.

FAIR USE

According to the U.S. Copyright Office, "the doctrine of fair use has developed through a substantial number of court decisions over the years and has been codified in section 107 of the copyright law." It provides for various uses for which reproduction without seeking permission may be fair and lists the factors to determine if a particular use is fair. These include:

- The purpose and character of the use, including whether such use is of commercial nature or is for nonprofit educational purposes
- The nature of the copyrighted work
- The amount and substantiality of the portion used in relation to the copyrighted work as a whole
- The effect of the use upon the potential market for, or value of, the copyrighted work

There is no easy or foolproof way to determine what is fair use, and no safe amount of text or use of a photograph that clearly falls within its parameters. Moreover, acknowledgment of copyrighted material does not replace the need to obtain permission. Litigation is the ultimate determiner of what is fair use and what is infringement. When in doubt, consult an attorney.[17]

PLAGIARISM

Plagiarism is use of another writer's words as your own. It does not necessarily involve copyright infringement, since the question of whether or not a work is protected by copyright does not matter. Recent scandals involving prominent historians have helped to bring attention to the issue and the importance of historical documentation. In his interesting and useful look at the topic, *The Little Book of Plagiarism*, Richard A. Posner distinguishes between fair use and plagiarism:

> The fair-use doctrine permits quotation of brief passages from a copyrighted work without the copyright holder's permission. . . . But the fair user is assumed to use quotation marks and credit the source; he is not a plagiarist. . . . The law does not excuse copyright infringement, no matter how fulsome the infringer's acknowledgment of his copying; but the acknowledgment will exonerate him of any charge of plagiarism. . . . Concealment is at the heart of plagiarism.

While careful note taking and accurate documentation may prove no ultimate protection for copyright infringement, they can provide protection against charges of plagiarism, which is an even surer destroyer of reputations and careers.[18]

Historical writing, like any other skill, requires dedication, study, and diligent practice in order to improve. Like John Adams's journey to the Continental Congress, it is not for the weak of heart or mind. Nevertheless, as with any endeavor that is worthwhile, the successful writer of local history will be amply rewarded for overcoming the obstacles and challenges of effective communication, primarily with the deep learning and understanding that accompanies research and writing. English author E. M. Forster is often quoted as asking, "How can I tell what I think till I see what I say?"[19] Only by fully engaging in the research and writing process can one ever come close to knowing what one thinks, understanding the past in any profound way, and attaining the kind of knowledge that is truly its own reward.

NOTES

1. John Ruston Pagan, *Anne Orthwood's Bastard: Sex and Law in Early Virginia* (New York: Oxford University Press, 2003), 8–9.

2. Pagan, *Anne Orthwood's Bastard*, 9–10.

3. Pagan, *Anne Orthwood's Bastard*, 115.

4. Nathaniel Philbrick, *In the Heart of the Sea: The Tragedy of the Whaleship* Essex (New York: Viking, 2000), xii–xiii.

5. Michael Gross, *Genuine Authentic: The Real Life of Ralph Lauren* (New York: HarperCollins, 2003), xii–xii, xvi.

6. Christopher B. Coleman, preface to Donald Dean Parker, *Local History: How to Gather It, Write It, and Publish It*, rev. and ed. Bertha E. Josephson for the Committee on Guide for Study of Local History of the Social Science Research Council (New York: SSRC, 1944), x. Coleman was director of the Indiana Historical Bureau; Parker was head of the Department of History and Political Science at what is now South Dakota State University at Brookings; Josephson was on the staff at what is now the Ohio Historical Society and a member of the AASLH's Editorial Board.

7. Mark Twain, *The Tragedy of Pudd'nhead Wilson* (Hartford, Conn.: American Publishing Company, 1894), 130.

8. "Library Resource Guides: Brown University Library," http://library.brown.edu/gateway/lrg.php?id=30&task=topic&topic_id=94 (accessed January 9, 2013).

9. Thomas E. Felt, *Researching, Writing, and Publishing Local History* (1976; 2nd ed., Nashville, Tenn.: American Association for State and Local History, 1981), 68–69.

10. George Geib, "Development and Preservation," *Traces of Indiana and Midwestern History* 11, no. 1 (Winter 1999): 52–53.

11. Richard Marius and Melvin E. Page, *A Short Guide to Writing about History* (1989; 8th ed., Boston: Pearson, 2012), 116.

12. Eric Pace, "Barbara Tuchman Dead at 77; A Pulitzer-Winning Historian," *New York Times*, February 7, 1989.

13. National Endowment for the Humanities, "David McCullough Interview," www.neh.gov/about/awards/jefferson-lecture/david-mccullough-interview (accessed August 30, 2012).

14. David McCullough, *John Adams* (New York: Simon and Schuster, 2001), 17–18.

15. Marius and Page, *A Short Guide to Writing about History*, 119–20.

16. Edward Samuels, *The Illustrated Story of Copyright* (New York: Thomas Dunne Books, 2000).

17. "U.S. Copyright Office: Fair Use," www.copyright.gov/fls/fl102.html (accessed January 9, 2013).

18. Richard A. Posner, *The Little Book of Plagiarism* (New York: Pantheon, 2007), 16–17.

19. E. M. Forster, *Aspects of the Novel* (New York: Harcourt, Brace and Company, 1927), 101.

FOUR

Economics, Design, and Production: How Do You Produce and Market a Book That People Will Pay For? (Publishing)

You have identified the target or core audience that you hope to reach. You have researched, written, and revised your draft publication. Now you are ready to publish. Publication is a multifaceted process involving at least seven major elements: acquisition, editing, design (including composition), dissemination (print or electronic), storage and order fulfillment (if your publication is printed), marketing (promotion and publicity), and sales.

ACQUISITION

If you are an author, you will need to decide whether to self-publish or to contract with a publisher. If you are a publisher (state or local historical society or small press), you will need to contract with an author. Authors submitting proposals and manuscripts should study the websites and catalogs of publishers to ensure that their submissions reflect a solid understanding of publishers' lists of titles and the goals that the publishers are seeking to accomplish (on these matters, see the section on "Preliminary Manuscript Preparation" in chapter 3). A good proposal letter will reflect that the author is aware of the publisher's list, the audience it seeks to reach, and why the book being proposed would be a good addition. The proposal should also indicate particular groups or organizations of which the author is a member or has special access to for marketing purposes, information about the author's credentials and previous publications, and a sample table of contents and chapter if available. Finally, the editor will want to know when the manuscript will be finished and if the author is submitting to other publishers simultaneously. While simultaneous submission has traditionally been frowned upon in the world of publishing (especially among peer-reviewed publishers because of the labor intensity of peer review), it is generally accepted today on the condition that the author acknowledges it upon submission.

The legal liabilities of author and publisher are sufficiently complex that a contract, or publisher's agreement, needs to define their relationship. The basic issues to be agreed upon include acceptance (sometimes, in the case of university presses or other kinds of not-for-profit publishers, contingent upon approval by an editorial advisory board or board of directors); compensation in terms of a lump-sum payment, royalties, advances on royalties, free copies, and/or discounts for additional copies; warranties that the author's work is original, that it has not been published before, and that the author has the right to assign copyright in the work (including responsibility for acquiring necessary permissions for any use of the work of others, i.e., third-party content, that appears in the work); assignment of copyright; assurance that the author will not be publishing another competing book; and designation of the period following formal acceptance by which the book will be published. (Sample publishing agreements appear in appendixes 2 and 3.)

When self-publishing or contracting with a nonprofit publisher, an author of a book on local history will receive modest if any compensation. Such an author—especially if previously unpublished—should not have unrealistic expectations of compensation through royalties. Authors should be aware that because local history books do not have large audiences, the royalties they earn—if any—will be very low. Many publishers now ask authors to waive royalties on the first five hundred copies of the work or entirely. Authors, local libraries, or historical societies should not embark on a book publishing project in the expectation of making money.

A publisher, when accepting a book for publication, takes on the investment risk on that book. In deciding to publish, the publisher makes a business decision that the expense, time, and effort to publish will be compensated by the sales income for the book. Even nonprofit presses do this calculation, and many worthy projects are turned away because the publisher does not wish to take this risk.

Negotiations sometimes break down over the indemnification clause, whereby the author indemnifies and holds harmless the publisher in case of lawsuits that involve a breach of the author's warranties and representations—notably the warranty that the work is original—in other words, in case of infringement of copyright. An author needs to understand that this is a standard contract feature that provides one more incentive to avoid infringement of copyright and plagiarism.

Whether you are an author or a publisher, you should seek the advice of a lawyer. You will need not just any general practice lawyer but a lawyer who specializes in intellectual property and copyright law. A lawyer who can keep you out of court will have earned his or her fee. A state or local historical society that acts as a publisher, or a small press, will have frequent recourse to a boilerplate (standard or sample) contract and, in consultation with an intellectual property lawyer, should work out such a boilerplate contract to use with authors.

A fundamental early decision in the publication process is who shall own the copyright of the publication. A publisher who wants to own all rights to the publication should be ready to pay more, either in a lump sum or in royalties, to an author. The publisher will thereby assume the accompanying responsibilities, including placing the copyright notice in the book, registering the publication with the United States Copyright Office, and supplying necessary copies for deposit. Publishers are often in the best position to manage subsidiary rights, such as foreign rights, translation rights, serial rights, paperback rights, motion picture rights, and electronic rights. While local historians working with small publishers are not likely to be concerned to a significant degree with subsidiary rights issues, movie options and translations are sometimes desired, and authors should be aware of the possibilities. With the rise in popularity of e-books, electronic rights are increasingly considered as basic publishing rights and subject to primary royalty.[1]

An author who wants to retain copyright, and a publisher who wants to reduce payments to an author, can agree on a license (exclusive or nonexclusive) to publish. An agreement whereby an author grants to a publisher a license to publish that is exclusive for a certain period or for so long as the publisher keeps the publication in print, and then converts to a nonexclusive license, can be mutually advantageous. The website of the Copyright Information Center at Cornell University provides a good list of the options available to authors confronted with these choices, as well as sample language and video tutorials that provide advice.[2] Another site that will be of interest to those needing to make decisions about what rights to retain and what to grant to a publisher is the Scholar's Copyright Addendum Engine, which offers various options for an author to select and then generates a printable addendum that can be submitted to a publisher.[3]

For an author or a publisher embarking on a first-time or only-time publication, acquisition is a one-off prospect. But for authors and publishers for whom publishing will be a long-term enterprise, acquisition becomes an activity requiring a long-term commitment of time and resources. In the case of the publisher, that commitment becomes a responsibility carried out by editors. Acquisition is essentially a networking activity—authors seeking a publisher, and acquisition editors seeking authors, networking through professional societies. In the field of local history, networking takes place through state and local historical societies and professional organizations such as the American Association for State and Local History.

EDITING

Every author needs an editor. Every manuscript can be improved by the application of another set of eyes. The publication process is not only a networking but also a collegial activity. An author should ask trusted colleagues in the field to read and critique a draft publication. Readers who serve as representatives of the intended audience can also provide useful commentary. Once manuscripts are submitted, historical societies and university presses use peer review as a method of quality control. Thus submissions should receive critiques by both inside readers chosen by the author and outside readers chosen by the publisher. In the "double-blind" peer review system, outside readers are anonymous, and the identity of the author is withheld from the reader. After a commitment is made to publish, some but not all outside reviewers are willing to be made known to the author and enter into a collaborative revision process.

The publisher may request or require revision before publication. The publisher may make a commitment to publish contingent on revision. After publisher and author agree to publish, and the text more or less ceases to be a moving target, the publication is ready for copyediting.

Just as an author's best ally is a knowledgeable archivist or reference librarian during the research phase of a project, so during the publication phase an author's most valuable ally is a skilled copy editor. Ideally the copy editor will be knowledgeable in not only language and style conventions but also the historical content of the publication. Marshall Lee, in his excellent in-depth treatment of all phases of publishing, *Bookmaking: Editing/Design/Production*, details the various functions of copyediting, including correcting typographical errors, errors of fact, errors of grammar, improving awkward sentences, enforcing conformity to the house style, and marking the manuscript for composition and design. "Copyeditors often go well beyond these efforts," he explains, "revising the structure and even sequence of chapters. . . . There is nothing wrong with this provided that the author and the editor are willing, and the copyeditor is competent."[4] An author will be lucky if the publisher can provide copyediting service. No press that we are aware of today provides source checking; few publishers today provide fact checking. When published reviews expose errors in a publication, the publisher's response is usually that factual accuracy is the author's responsibility. Fortunate is the author who forges a productive working relationship with the publisher's copy editor.

Whether or not a copy editor will be available to work on a publication, authors should immerse themselves during the writing phase in the style convention (for example *The Chicago Manual of Style* or the *Associated Press Stylebook*; see chapter 3) that will be used in editing the publication. The cleaner the author can make the manuscript before editing, the less editing the manuscript will require, and fewer disagreements between author and editor will ensue. In the memorable words of *The Economist Style Guide*: "Scrupulous writers will also notice that their copy is edited only lightly and is likely to be used. It may even be read."[5] During the editing and production phases, beware of typographical errors in unexpected areas of a publication where a proofreader's guard may be down, such as the cover, the spine, and the title page.

DESIGN

Computers have revolutionized all phases of publication, not least in the area of design. In all publication areas, computerization has forced on to authors and publishers activities formerly performed by contractors, none more so than in the areas of composition and design. The good news is that opportunities for publishing are greater now than at any time during the past. If authors or publishers choose to take on themselves the tasks of composition and design, they can dramatically reduce the costs of publication. The bad news—if it can be called that—is that these tasks are labor intensive and time consuming.

Publishing incurs two general types of cost: fixed and variable. Fixed costs include research, writing, editing, design, and composition. Design and composition are now called prepress in the electronic age. Fixed costs are present—whether or not borne gratis by the author—for both electronic publications and printed books. Design includes composition (typesetting and page layout [composed of aspects such as the sizing and placing of graphic elements—illustrations, maps, and charts]). All these fixed-cost functions are now computerized in one way or another. Variable costs depend on the number of copies printed (printing, paper, binding, and storage) or the number of copies sold (royalties to the author). The only savings that electronic publishing (such as on the Web) can realize (assuming that the electronic publication is well designed) is the fixed costs of printing, paper, binding, and storage. These savings are often offset by the costs of data conversion to files appropriate for e-readers. The term desktop publishing is a misnomer: It should more accurately be called desktop composition. Authors or publishers who choose to do design themselves can apply QuarkXPress or Adobe InDesign. These are sophisticated software programs intended for professional book designers and run on Macintosh or Microsoft Windows operating systems.

Electronic publishing has opened wide possibilities for authors and historical organizations and transformed the publishing industry. But a computer with its unlimited options for fonts and visual effects will not make a user who knows little about design into a talented and effective designer of books or websites. Good design is an important component of a successful publication, and authors working with commercial presses or university presses will have opportunities to suggest possible cover ideas and to comment on the suitability of cover and page design. The ultimate decision in these matters, however, lies with the publisher, who will likely have the best understanding of how to reach the book's intended market. Many presses will have a style and format already developed for a series, and authors will need to work within the parameters already established by the publisher. Local historical organizations seeking to bring out a book for commemorative or other purposes should seek a designer with some experience in book design. Designers will charge a rate based on a per-page cost and determined by the use of color and the number of illustrations. Publishers want from authors files in Word for Windows, or application files that they can edit and manipulate, not as PDF (portable document format) files, before sending them to the compositor. When a publication is ready, the publisher sends the made-up pages to the printer on a flash drive or uploaded from an FTP (file transfer protocol) site.

With the dramatic rise in the ownership of electronic devices for reading e-books, including smartphones, tablets, and dedicated e-book readers, e-books have become a commonplace and expected piece of the publishing equation. While the variable costs of print, paper, and binding are not necessary for e-book production, other production costs for converting print files to standard e-book files come into play. Many conversion services exist to accommodate the growing demand, and rates and quality can vary widely. Conversion houses can accommodate a wide variety of files, including Microsoft Word, PDF, Quark, InDesign, and many others. They can also scan printed books and provide digital files for e-book distribution. The most common files for e-book production are Mobipocket/Kindle files and ePub files. Mobipocket is a French company that got an early start on e-book creation and was bought by Amazon in 2005. Mobipocket files are for books read on Amazon's Kindle readers and apps (mobile applications that allow Kindle books to be read on any device). The ePub format is a standard for the industry maintained by the International Digital Publishing Forum, a nonprofit organization composed of publishers and technology companies. The ePub format supports books that can be read on Windows and Mac computers, on the Barnes & Noble NOOK devices, Sony Readers, and Apple devices (iPad/iPhone/iPod Touch) in iBooks and in other apps.[6]

DISSEMINATION (PRINT OR ELECTRONIC)

Options for printing include photocopying (for short publications in short pressruns), digital printing (for short-run and print-on-demand publications), and offset lithography (for pressruns greater than about seven hundred copies). Options for binding include case bound/cloth bound (usually Smyth-sewn, for larger books), perfect bound/paperback (can be sewn—for greater durability—or glued), and saddle-stitched/stapled (for pamphlets of up to sixty pages).

The most cost-effective method of printing a short book in black and white is digital printing for the text and offset lithography for the cover (which allows for color), with extra covers for publicity and in case of a reprint or print on demand. Any book intended to be sold at retail in bookstores will need a color cover—a color offset lithography-printed cover for a paperback book or a color dust jacket for a clothbound book. Color is essential to sell a book at retail in a bookstore. Buyers really do judge a book by its cover, and traditional offset printing can ensure the highest quality, though digital color printing is rapidly improving and should not be ruled out entirely when planning a project. To protect copies from becoming shopworn on bookstore shelves, paperback covers need to be laminated, and hardback books with dust jackets need to be shrink wrapped.

When selecting a printer, an author or publisher should solicit multiple bids by means of a request for proposals (RFP). Sample requests for proposals appear in appendixes 5 and 7. A long-standing dictum of the printing trade is that a printer can offer three desiderata: quality, punctuality, and a good price. Of those three, the client may choose two.

Another custom of which the client should be aware (read the "conventions of the printing trade" that are often printed on the reverse side of contracts): most printing contracts allow the printer to supply 10 percent over or 10 percent under the number of copies specified in the contract, and the client is obligated to pay for the number of copies delivered. This is a vestige of the days when printing presses were difficult to stop. But in the twenty-first century, pressruns are more easily controllable, underruns are rare (but do occasionally occur), and overruns are common. If you require an absolute minimum number of copies (for instance, to supply subscribers or members of your organization), you should order a bit more than you need to allow for the possibility of an underrun, or have a candid conversation with your customer service representative about the number of copies that you actually need.

If your publication is a bound photocopy, for instance a family history, the audience for which is immediate family members and somewhat more broadly genealogical researchers, then you can donate copies to interested family members and genealogical libraries such as:

- The Family History Library at the Genealogical Society of Utah (the largest genealogical library in the United States), 50 East North Temple, Salt Lake City, Utah 84150-9001; (801) 538-2978; https://familysearch.org. The Family History Library website (https://familysearch.org/archives) provides step-by-step instructions on how to conduct family history research. The Family History Library, operated by the Church of Jesus Christ of Latter-day Saints (LDS Church), operates seventeen regional and thousands of local (ward, branch, and stake) Family History Centers throughout the United States and other countries.
- The Allen County Public Library (the second-largest genealogical library in the United States), 6600 East State Boulevard, Fort Wayne, Indiana 46815-7029; (260) 421-1320; www.acpl.lib.in.us.
- Your state library and your local public library.
- Your state historical society and your local/county historical society.

ESTIMATING COSTS AND SETTING THE LIST (RETAIL) PRICE OF A BOOK

Nonprofit publishers set the list (retail) price of their books at four to five times unit cost of production, in order to recover that unit cost after selling at discounts in the range of 50 percent to retailers and wholesalers. For-profit publishers set the list price at eight to ten times unit cost of production. For the details of calculating costs and setting the list price, see appendix 8 of this book: "Why Books Cost: A Quick Lesson in Finance for Publishers," by Gregory M. Britton.

GRANTS, SPONSORSHIPS, AND ADVERTISING

Publishing involves financial risks for costs that are incurred before any books are sold and any revenue is received. To mitigate such risks, especially for community-based projects or books that may involve high production costs due to the need for the use of color, special paper or binding, or a large number of illustrations, you may want to apply for a grant to support the expenses of your project. A logical funding prospect for a local history project is your local community development foundation. Another potential source of funding for local history publication projects is to sell sponsorships and/or space advertising in your publication to area companies—a long-standing practice extending from the county histories published during the nineteenth century to today's photo books assembled by packagers working with local historical societies funded by local companies.

STORAGE AND ORDER FULFILLMENT

The requirements of storage are one more incentive to contract with a full-service publisher or with an order-fulfillment company. Order fulfillment can be contracted out to a company that will warehouse the books and process and ship orders. The Chicago Distribution Center (CDC; 11030 South Langley Avenue, Chicago, Illinois 60628-3830; (773) 702-7010; www.press.uchicago.edu/cdc/services.html) is a major storage and order-fulfillment facility. The CDC maintains an inventory of 12 million books in a 270,000-square-foot facility and ships 19,000 units daily. Some self-publishing companies also provide storage and order-fulfillment services. But given the thin margins on which a small press operates, the fees for contracting out those services can possibly eliminate any chance of cost recovery without careful consideration of such factors as pressrun, the number of units printed, and pricing.

SELF-PUBLISHING

Self-publishing used to be a marginal activity, dismissed as "vanity publishing," even though university presses for many decades often imposed author subventions (or financial support, for books that might be expensive to produce because of the need for additional pages, color, or illustrations). But recently self-publishing has become a force driving growth in, and has entered the mainstream of, the publishing industry. Some 211,000 book titles were self-published in 2011, representing a 60 percent increase over 2010.

Before the advent of the digital age and the development of the current plethora of publishers working through Web interfaces and producing digital print-on-demand copies in low quantities and e-books, self-publishing was an expensive and labor-intensive exercise that often resulted in a garage full of books that never saw the shelves of a bookstore or the light of day. *The Culture and Commerce of Publishing in the 21st Century* offers a useful "Analysis of the Economics of Self-Publishing," which looks at the cost of producing 500 paperback copies of a 362-page, black-and-white book that used royalty-free art for a color cover. Costs were as follows: $5,000 for a commercial printer using traditional lithographic equipment ranging down to $1,875 for a digital printer who specializes in books. Self-publishers in the past also had to bear the cost of creating relationships with booksellers, purchasing ISBNs (International Standard Book Number, a unique number required for books to be ordered by bookstores or libraries), handling fulfillment, and creating promotional materials.[7]

The new crop of self-publishers, however, offers a wide range of packages to suit the needs and the budgets of a diverse array of authors. On the low end, the publishers will produce a certain number of books based on the files that an author submits. In addition, publishers offer packages that can include all the tasks that were so formidable for self-publishers in the past, such as ISBN registration, copy editing, proofreading, cover design, page layout, distribution, marketing, and management of sales and returns.

Authors and small presses can self-publish through manufacturing-on-demand publishers such as:

- CreateSpace, 7290 Investment Drive, Unit B, Charleston, South Carolina 29418-8305 (for books); www.createspace.com. A subsidiary of Amazon.com, CreateSpace is a manufacturing-on-demand publisher of books, DVDs, video downloads, and MP3s.
- Lightning Source, Inc., 1246 Heil Quaker Boulevard, La Vergne, Tennessee 37086-3515; (615) 213-5815; inquiry@lightning source.com; www.lightningsource.com.
- The subsidiaries, all at 1663 South Liberty Drive, Bloomington, Indiana 47404-5161, of Author Solutions, Inc., the largest self-publishing company in the world:
  - AuthorHouse, (888) 519-5121; authorsupport@authorhouse .com; www.authorhouse.com.
  - iUniverse, Inc., (800) 288-4677; www.iuniverse.com.
  - Xlibris Corporation, (888) 795-4274; publishtoday@xlibris .com; www.xlibris.com.

The enhanced standing of self-publishing was demonstrated in 2012 when the Penguin Group (a subsidiary of Pearson, based in London) purchased Author Solutions. The purchase of Author Solutions is evidence of a new direction in the publishing industry. Tony Cook, business correspondent for the *Indianapolis Star*, predicts that mainstream publishers will use self-publishing subsidiaries "as a kind of screening process funded by the writers." Michael Norris, a senior analyst at Simba Information, a market research firm, observes, "I think that Pearson is going to go through this with a fine-tooth comb and identify the ones that are going to appeal to a wider audience." But authors and small presses considering self-publishing should do so with their eyes open. Self-publishing companies do not disclose the sales records of their titles. Throughout the publishing industry, only about 7 percent of all book titles, and about 5 percent of self-published book titles, sell more than a thousand copies.[8]

WRITING AND PUBLISHING LOCAL HISTORY ON THE WEB

Websites provide a cost effective means for distributing various kinds of historical content, including family histories, conference proceedings, and research tools such as cumulative indexes for historical periodicals and primary sources. They can also accommodate multimedia, such as film, video, audio recordings, and music, in ways that are impossible in a printed book. Users interact with websites, or navigate, in individual ways along paths that correspond to their interests and inclinations and not in a linear fashion as they might with a print publication. Moreover, the majority of visitors are likely to be directed to a part of the site from a search engine and not necessarily to a home page, or landing page, of the site. Therefore, website architecture and navigation are primary considerations that must be planned carefully. As Jenny L. Presnell explains, "Architecture in this sense is not the programming of the website but, rather, how it is laid out, labeled, and organized, as well as how visitors will navigate through it."[9]

There are many books available as guides to commercial website design, such as Patrick J. Lynch and Sarah Horton's *Web Style Guide*, Louis Rosenfeld and Peter Morville's *Information Architecture for the World Wide Web*, and Steve Krug's *Don't Make Me Think: A Common Sense Approach to Web Usability*.[10] These books are useful for historians seeking advice about how to make their websites user friendly. One of the most important books dealing specifically with presenting history on the Web is Daniel J. Cohen and Roy Rosenzweig's *Digital History: A Guide to Gathering, Preserving, and Presenting the Past on the Web*. The book exists in both a print version and a digital version that can be accessed for free and is the first book to be consulted for those wanting to enter the field of digital history.[11]

Cohen and Rosenzweig take readers on a tour of the "History Web," discussing its development and highlighting the different genres of sites that exist along with significant examples. "From the perspective of those who are thinking about creating their own website, probably the most helpful way to classify history websites is by the types of materials they provide and the functions and audiences they serve," the authors explain. "The past decade has seen the emergence of five main genres of history websites that follow preexisting patterns and categories; archives (containing primary sources); exhibits, films, scholarship, and essays (that is, secondary sources); teaching (directed at students and teachers); discussion (focused on online dialogue); and organizational (providing information about a historical group). Yet these categories are often loosely followed and frequently blurred." For example, organizational sites often contain primary sources, interpretative essays, and teaching materials along with information about the hours they are open and explanations of mission and programs. Despite the fact that websites seldom conform to one genre, thinking about genres helps one to consider "how what you are doing relates to the audience you are hoping to reach."[12]

Creators of sites should review examples that reflect the type of site they wish to emulate, examining the nature of the page design, navigation, organization, and the text. How easy is it to move around in the site without getting lost? Is navigation logical and intuitive? Are the same buttons on every page in the same place? Is the design inviting or distracting? For large sites, is there a "breadcrumb trail" to help visitors see where they are in the site and find their way back to where they came from? Are the hyperlinks obvious, or are they difficult to detect? All of these considerations and more must be taken into account to build a website that users will want to return to and that others will link to, thereby increasing the likelihood of showing up high on search results pages.

In *The Information-Literate Historian*, Jenny L. Presnell provides a list of necessary components for a website to be taken seriously:

- Biographical information about the author—a component of establishing a site's credibility.
- Statement of purpose—very helpful in evaluating the authority and usefulness of a site.
- Contact link for questions—to enhance discussion and to identify errors and broken links.
- Last updated date—to identify how active a site is and how well it is maintained.
- A title—at the top of each page so visitors will know where they are.
- Metadata—terms that describe the site so visitors can find it.[13]

In addition to titles mentioned above, the following publications provide excellent discussion of encoding and design for electronic publications:

- Elizabeth Castro, *EPUB, Straight to the Point: Creating Ebooks for the Apple iPad and Other eReaders* (Berkeley, Calif.: Peachpit Press, 2011).
- Cyndi Howells, *Planting Your Family Tree Online: How to Create Your Own Family History Web Site* (Nashville, Tenn.: Rutledge Hill Press, 2004), www.cyndislist.com/planting.
- Jakob Nielsen, *Designing Web Usability: The Practice of Simplicity* (Indianapolis: New Riders Publishing, 1999), www.useit.com.
- Bob Trubshaw [R. W. Trubshaw], *How to Write and Publish Local and Family History Successfully: Books, Booklets, Magazines, CD-ROMs, and Web Sites* (1999; rev. ed., Loughborough, U.K.: Heart of Albion Press, 2005).

BLOGS, BLOGGING, AND SOCIAL MEDIA

"Blog," a term derived from the conflation of "Web log," is an online journal to which the "blogger" contributes regularly, offering opinion and commentary and often including multimedia components. Blogs began appearing in the late 1990s but really became prevalent in the 2000s, having a major impact on journalism, politics, and scholarship. According to Cohen and Rosenzweig, John Barger, the proprietor of the *Robot Wisdom Weblog*, originated the term in 1997, and the blog as personal journal became popular among young people working in technology companies in the late nineties. As blogs became more popular, software packages arose that greatly simplified the task of creating and maintaining a blog.[14] Current popular blog services include WordPress, Blogger, Xanga, and LiveJournal, among many others. The best are user friendly and inexpensive, often offering packages that are free. Blogs are generally written in an informal tone and should be updated frequently to be effective. According to Tim Grove, writing in the *Encyclopedia of Local History*, "the first requirement of a successful blog is commitment. . . . A blog that does not show recent activity will lose readers very quickly."[15] For authors, blogs can be a powerful tool for promoting books and ideas, bypassing the traditional gatekeepers of journalism and scholarship. But those that reflect the standards of careful writing along with creativity and timeliness will attract the most readers.

Michael J. Maddigan, a local historian blogger, says he began writing the blog Recollecting Nemasket "for two principal reasons: as a means of personal fulfillment and as an effort to make local history more readily available to the community." For him, digital publishing through a blog offers advantages that are not available through traditional publishing:

> Digital publishing is less restrictive, it permits me to publish longer works, more technical works, works with more images, portions of longer works that I have yet to complete—essentially whatever I choose. A website may also be used as a "proving ground" where articles can be subjected to criticism and comment before they are published elsewhere.
>
> I find that digital scholarship is also advantageous because it is more immediate, more interactive, more accessible, and less ephemeral than traditional publishing. It is also less expensive. My blog costs me nothing beyond the time that I put into it. Readers can read my posts as they are published and respond to them nearly instantaneously, providing feedback on what I write and occasionally offering a differing perspective. With traditional publishing, the process of receiving feedback is much more arduous. And unlike traditional scholarship published in books, magazines, and journals, digital scholarship does not necessarily go out of print or become unavailable when the next issue is published.[16]

One of the first things a visitor notices upon visiting Maddigan's blog (http://nemasket.blogspot.com) is how the images of photographs, paintings, and postcards related to the history of a particular place are beautifully displayed against the black background. Second is the statement of purpose: "Recollecting Nemasket is a web log about the history of Middleborough and Lakeville, Massachusetts. In addition to publishing local history articles, Recollecting Nemasket seeks to be an interactive educational resource for community history by providing links to historical information and sources, and by soliciting input from readers in the form of recollections, photographs and other images." Third, the site offers images of the author's printed books and links to ordering information. Finally, in addition to the reader's comments on the blog itself and a "contact me" link, the blog links to social media sites, such as Facebook and Google+, to direct the reader to other locations where dialogue, discussion, and communication about the area can continue.[17]

Blogs and social media can work together to build communities around and increase sales of printed books. Jerry Apps of Wisconsin, the author of more than thirty books on local history, is a deft manager of a variety of social media tools to promote his speaking engagements and printed books. His website (www.jerryapps.com) provides links to his blog and his social media accounts on Facebook and Twitter along with contact information and a great deal of information about his life and work. He provides an example to emulate for all aspiring local history authors.

In her article on social media for the *Encyclopedia of Local History*, Linda Norris gives this succinct definition: "Social media is Web-based technology designed to turn the Internet from a one-way form of communication into a dialogue." She acknowledges that it "is constantly changing, and the use of it by local history organizations continues to evolve."[18] The primary social media sites relevant to local historians as of this writing, in addition to the blog services previously mentioned, are Facebook, Twitter, and Flickr, though there are many more. *Wikipedia* lists more than two hundred.[19] For authors of local history, these platforms offer new ways to communicate with audiences of all ages and interests, and they are an absolute necessity for those wanting to sell books.

MARKETING

If your publication is Web-based, you should take steps to publicize its availability. Logical media are newsletters, periodicals, listservs, websites of sponsoring organizations and affinity groups such as state and local historical societies, and the Discussion Groups of H-Net, Humanities and Social Sciences Online (www2.h-net.msu.edu).

If you have self-published a book—whether produced by a traditional printer, an electronic printer, or a print-on-demand company—you will need to market and sell the book yourself. One method of marketing and selling—whether a book is published by an individual or a state or local historical society or other small press—is by subscription in advance of publication. A number of companies—"packagers," as they are known in the book trade—work with local historical organizations to research, write, design, print, and sell books on local history topics. Often these are photo books with minimal text beyond caption information on the photos. Examples of such packagers include:

- Arcadia Publishing Company, 420 Wando Park Boulevard, Mount Pleasant, South Carolina 29464-7845; (843) 853-2070; www. arcadiapublishing.com.
- Donning Company Publishers, 184 Business Park Drive, Suite 206, Virginia Beach, Virginia 23462-6533; (800) 296-8572; www.donning. com.
- The History Press, 645 Meeting Street, Suite 200, Charleston, South Carolina 29403-4280; (843) 577-5971; http://historypress.net.

You can do the marketing and selling yourself. These tasks are labor-intensive and time-consuming. But whether your book is self-published or published by a state or local historical society or a small press, sales cannot be cost-effectively subcontracted or outsourced to a distributor. State and local historical societies and small presses have found that marketing and/or distribution agreements with larger publishers are rarely cost effective. "In the field of local history publishing," notes Bob Trubshaw, "the publisher *must* be the salesperson."[20] Distributors simply do not have the detailed knowledge of the contents of your book or of its likely market, nor do they have the financial incentive (no matter how high the percentage of net revenue received), to represent your book to retailers and individual book-buyers as effectively as a state or local historical publisher.

Marketing and sales tasks include communicating with and making personal visits to managers of bookstores and other retailers, who will expect you to discount the book to them at rates of 40 to 50 percent or more off the list (retail) price of the book, whether those bookstores and other retailers are for-profit or not-for-profit, such as museum stores. A retailer may be willing to sell your book on a consignment basis. You should be aware of the convention of returns in the book trade: An order is not a sale, and retailers reserve the right (often exercised) to return unsold books. In 2005 book-return rates were 35 percent for adult trade hardcovers, 22 percent for adult trade paperbacks, 17 percent for university press hardcovers, and 15 percent for university press paperbacks.[21] Retailers will sometimes accept books on a no-return basis, which requires a much deeper discount.

When self-publishing your book, you will need to advertise it in "earned" (free) media when you can get it, paid when you have to. Likely advertising media include the same newsletters, periodicals, listservs, and websites of sponsoring organizations and affinity groups such as state and local historical societies that you considered as venues to announce the availability of your publication. Consider paid advertising in newspapers local to the topic of your book and periodicals with readers likely to be interested in your book.

A good form of "earned" (free) media is a book review. You will need to send review copies of your book to the book review editor (addressed by name when possible, which will involve research) of local newspapers and periodicals publishing in the field of your book. The Discussion Groups of H-Net, Humanities and Social Sciences Online (www2.h-net. msu.edu) publish online reviews, so get to know the Discussion Groups of H-Net in your field. H-Net has individual Discussion Groups for seventeen states, the District of Columbia, and the following specialized topics relevant to readers and authors interested in local history:

H-Appalachia: Appalachian History and Studies
H-Borderlands: Spanish/Mexican Borderlands of the American South-
    west and Northern Mexico
H-Local: State and Local History; Museums
H-NewEngland: New England History and Culture
H-OralHist: Studies Related to Oral History
H-Public: Public History
H-Rural: Rural and Agricultural History
H-South: History of the United States South
H-West: History and Culture of the North American West and Fron-
    tiers

Always check to make sure that a newspaper or periodical reviews books (a declining feature) in your field, to reduce the possibility of wasting review copies. Newspapers review books quickly, but academic journals can take a year or more to publish a review, by which time such a review will have a minimal effect on sales unless yours is a book that academic libraries will purchase. Most books—except for the fortunate few perennial sellers—sell as much as 90 percent of their lifetime sales during the first year following publication.

Before the book goes to the printer:

- Apply for an International Standard Book Number (ISBN) from R. R. Bowker, the official United States ISBN agency (www.isbn.org/standards/home/index.asp). The ISBN is a unique thirteen-digit commercial book identifier. The single most important thing to do in publishing today is getting accurate, thorough, and timely metadata (the unique descriptors of a publication, such as the ISBN and the Cataloging in Publication record) to online vendors, wholesalers, and distributors. This is the publisher's responsibility, but self-publishers are at a distinct disadvantage if they do not heed this. This is how Amazon.com gets a book and detailed description into its system.

- Apply for a Cataloging in Publication (CIP) record from the Library of Congress (www.loc.gov/publish/cip). When the book is published, the publisher includes the CIP data on the copyright page, thereby facilitating book processing for libraries and book dealers.
- Register the copyright with the United States Copyright Office (www.copyright.gov/eco). This involves, among other things, sending copies for deposit. Without registration, you can successfully defend your rights of authorship against an infringer in court, but with registration, you will have an open-and-shut case.

About the time that the book goes to the printer:

- Compile a review media list with the name, address, and other contact information of the book review editor for each newspaper, periodical, or broadcaster.
- Compile a list with addresses and other contact information of bookstores, convention and visitors associations, chambers of commerce, and museums local to the subject of your book. See the *ABA Bookseller Member Directory*: www.bookweb.org/aba/members/search.do. This is a directory of the bookseller members of the American Booksellers Association; it is a database, searchable by location and specialty categories.
- Prepare press releases. The press release should include full details on the author, title, summary of contents, size of the book, number of pages, number of illustrations, type of binding, ISBN number, name of the imprint, how to order, and price.
- Send press releases to your list of bookstores, convention and visitors associations, chambers of commerce, and museums local to the subject of your book.
- Allow four to six weeks between the delivery date promised by the printer and scheduling the launch date, especially if you plan a launch party, to allow reviews to appear in newspapers and to allow for late delivery of books from the printer.

At least three months before launch:

If your book has a chance of national sales, send advance page proofs of the book to prepublication book trade review media:

- *Booklist*, American Library Association, 50 East Huron Street, Chicago, Illinois 60611-2788. For submission guidelines, see www.booklistonline.com/get-reviewed.
- *ForeWord*, Book Review Editor, 425 Boardman Avenue, Suite B, Traverse City, Michigan 49684-2562. Reviews independently published books. Submission guidelines: www.forewordreviews.com/services/book-reviews.
- *Kirkus Reviews*, 479 Old Carolina Court, Mount Pleasant, South Carolina 29464-7823 (for adult nonfiction). Submission guidelines:

www.kirkusreviews.com/about/submission-guidlines. If your book is self-published, see information on the Kirkus Indie Program at www.kirkusreviews.com/indie/about.

- *Library Journal*, Book Review Editor, 160 Varick Street, 11th Floor, New York, New York 10013-1220. Submission guidelines: http://reviews.libraryjournal.com/about/submitting-titles-for-review.
- *Midwest Book Review*, 278 Orchard Drive, Oregon, WI 53575-1129. Submission guidelines: www.midwestbookreview.com/get_rev.htm. An excellent list of book review media: www.midwestbookreview.com/bookbiz/advice/bkrevmag.htm.
- *Publishers Weekly*, Nonfiction Reviews, 71 West 23rd Street, Suite 1608, New York, NY 10010-4186. Submission guidelines: www.publishersweekly.com/pw/corp/submissionguidelines.html. If your book is self-published, see information on the PW Select Program at www.publishersweekly.com/pw/diy/index.html.

Two months before launch:

- Write/publish promotional articles about the book.
- Excerpt chapters from the book in periodicals.

On delivery of books from the printer:

- Carefully inspect several sample copies to ensure that there are no unpleasant surprises.

One month before launch:

- Make sure that bookstores have copies before articles/interviews about the book appear in local media.
- Send press releases to monthly and weekly periodicals.
- Send out review copies, together with a press release and a personalized cover letter, to review media.
- Schedule interviews with the author(s) in local media (daily newspapers and radio and television stations), to coincide with launch.
- Organize launch party.

One week before launch:

- Send press releases to media (daily newspapers and radio and television stations).

At the time of launch:

- Interviews (previously scheduled) with the author(s) in local media (daily newspapers and radio and television stations).

At a launch party:

- Have photographs taken for later publicity use.

After the launch:

- Follow up with local media (daily newspapers and radio and television stations).
- Arrange author talks and book signings.
- Arrange follow-up, spinoff, and promotional articles related to the subject of the book to appear in specialist periodicals.

SALES

The decline and demise of independent bookstores pose a challenge to publishing in the field of local history. Mass-market chain bookstores have squeezed and driven many independent bookstores out of business. Even Borders, a major mass-market bookstore, went bankrupt and out of business in 2011. The chains demand and get high discounts and often pay invoices after ninety days or more. A small local history publisher is at the mercy of the retailer (whether independent or mass-market chain), who will allocate little shelf space to local history titles. So—encourage retail bookstore sales in any way that you can, but the bulk of sales for a self-publishing author, a state or local historical society, or a small press will come from direct orders.

Self-publishing authors can list and sell their books on Amazon.com, and a small press can become an Amazon affiliate. As soon as the book appears on Amazon the author should set up an Amazon author page. Amazon allows customers to preorder books and also to "like" a forthcoming book. Because books with high numbers of "likes" can effect Amazon's initial purchasing of the book, authors might encourage friends and colleagues to do so. Authors can also promote this on their Facebook or Twitter accounts. Since the author is driving attention to the book, this is an acceptable—even desirable—practice. This should not be confused with anonymously reviewing one's own book, which is unethical and violates Amazon's rules. Encouraging others to post reviews on Amazon is perfectly acceptable. Here too books with heavy review traffic are treated more favorably by search engines and appear higher up on those searches.

THE ATTRACTIONS OF A FULL-SERVICE PUBLISHER

The foregoing sketch of the labor-intensive process of marketing a self-published book contrasts with the several advantages of contracting with a full-service publisher, who will do most or all of the marketing, advertising, distribution, and sales tasks, in addition to handling editing and production (design, composition, printing, and binding). Small presses are ideal for local-history subjects. Some full-service publishers encourage authors to sell copies themselves (copies purchased by the author at the author's cost). Other publishers do not want the author to compete with the publisher's retail operation, and so arrange for the authors to sell copies for the publisher's retail operation. A full-service publisher will coordinate the distribution of copies for review. Such a publisher will send to the author a marketing questionnaire asking the author to identify, among other things, journals in the field and local newspapers that will be likely media for reviewing and advertising the book. An author should thoroughly and punctually fill out and return such a questionnaire. Fortunate is the author who forges a productive working relationship with the publisher's marketing staff.

THE GOAL: COMMUNICATING NEW KNOWLEDGE OF LOCAL HISTORY

You have researched, written, published, and marketed your book. If you have accomplished these tasks well, you will have fulfilled the valuable service of creating new knowledge of local history and communicating it to your audience. The technical aspects of publishing—acquisition, editing, design, dissemination, storage, order fulfillment, marketing, and sales—all serve the ultimate goal of communicating new knowledge of history. Historical knowledge grows incrementally, and writers of history build on the foundations created by their predecessors. Each new generation discovers new evidence, asks new questions, and creates opportunities for a fresh look at perennial topics. New perspectives provide new insights about the past.

NOTES

1. *The Chicago Manual of Style* (1906; 16th ed., Chicago: University of Chicago Press, 2010), 179–84.

2. "Copyright Information Center," http://copyright.cornell.edu/policies/copy right_management.cfm (accessed January 10, 2013).

3. "Science Commons: Scholar's Copyright Agreement," http://scholars. sciencecommons.org (accessed January 10, 2013).

4. Marshall Lee, *Bookmaking: Editing/Design/Production* (1965; 3rd ed., New York: W. W. Norton, 2004), 99–100.

5. www.economist.com/styleguide/introduction (accessed July 14, 2012).

6. "eBook Architects—eBook Formats," http://ebookarchitects.com/conversions/ formats.php#mobi (accessed January 13, 2013).

7. Albert Greco, Clara Rodríguez, and Robert Wharton, *The Culture and Commerce of Publishing in the 21st Century* (Stanford, Calif.: Stanford Business Books, 2006), 154–55.

8. Tony Cook, "Self-Publishing Comes in from the Cold with Sale," *Indianapolis Star*, July 20, 2012, A-5.

9. Jenny L. Presnell, *The Information-Literate Historian: A Guide to Research for History Students* (2007; 2nd ed., New York: Oxford University Press, 2013), 301.

10. Patrick J. Lynch and Sarah Horton, *Web Style Guide: Basic Design Principles for Creating Web Sites* (1999; 3rd ed., New Haven, Conn.: Yale University Press, 2009); Peter Morville and Louis Rosenfeld, *Information Architecture for the World Wide Web: Designing Large-Scale Web Sites* (1998; 3rd ed., Sebastopol, Calif.: O'Reilly Media, 2006); Steve Krug, *Don't Make Me Think: A Common Sense Approach to Web Usability* (2000; 2nd ed., Berkeley, Calif.: New Riders, 2006).

11. Daniel Cohen and Roy Rosenzweig, *Digital History: A Guide to Gathering, Preserving, and Presenting the Past on the Web* (Philadelphia: University of Pennsylvania Press, 2005); "Digital History: A Guide to Gathering, Preserving, and Presenting the Past on the Web," http://chnm.gmu.edu/digitalhistory/ (accessed January 13, 2013).

12. Cohen and Rosenzweig, *Digital History*, 25.

13. Presnell, *The Information-Literate Historian*, 304–5.

14. Cohen and Rosenzweig, *Digital History*, 41.

15. Carol Kammen and Amy H. Wilson, eds., *Encyclopedia of Local History* (2000; 2nd ed., Lanham, Md.: AltaMira Press, 2013), 57.

16. Michael J. Maddigan, "Digital Scholar Profiles: 'Writing and Publishing Local History on the Web' | The Digital Scholar," www.thedigitalscholar.com/digital-scholars/michael-j-maddigan/ (accessed July 17, 2012).

17. Michael J. Maddigan, "Recollecting Nemasket," http://nemasket.blogspot.com (accessed January 14, 2013).

18. Kammen and Wilson, *Encyclopedia of Local History*, 504–6.

19. "List of Social Networking Websites—*Wikipedia*, the Free Encyclopedia," http://en.wikipedia.org/wiki/List_of_social_networking_websites (accessed January 14, 2013).

20. Bob Trubshaw, *How to Write and Publish Local and Family History Successfully: Books, Booklets, Magazines, CD-ROMs, and Web Sites* (Loughborough, U.K.: Heart of Albion Press, 2005), 241.

21. Greco, Rodríguez, and Wharton, *The Culture and Commerce of Publishing in the 21st Century*, 48.

Appendix 1: Sample Author's Guidelines

Published with permission of the Indiana Historical Society Press.

AUTHOR GUIDELINES

All prospective authors should read the Guidelines for All IHS Press Publications below, then refer to the author guidelines for the category or categories that best suit your work.

GUIDELINES FOR ALL IHS PRESS PUBLICATIONS

The following policy statement is intended to provide guidelines for potential authors and to set out the criteria used by IHS Press editors.

IHS Press publishes seven to nine new book titles per year, four issues of the popular history magazine *Traces*, two issues of the family history magazine *Connections* and two or more installments of articles and/or book-length pieces for *Online Connections*, published on the Web.

The IHS Press will issue a standard contract to an author on acceptance of a book-length manuscript or article for the magazines or *Online Connections*. Submission of a manuscript by an author or receipt of a manuscript by IHS Press shall not in any way be construed as an obligation by IHS Press to publish a manuscript.

IHS Press can make no commitment to publish until its editors can examine a completed manuscript with all notes and bibliography. The editors initially review manuscripts submitted for publication, then send suitable ones to appropriate outside readers for evaluation. Authors should allow 90 days or more for the evaluation process. The editors make the final decision for or against publishing a manuscript and reserve the right to edit accepted manuscripts to conform to IHS Press's style and usage.

Most acceptances are conditional on an author's revisions. After acceptance, the author is responsible for obtaining permission to reproduce any illustrations and for providing captions and credit lines for them. The author is also responsible for obtaining permission to publish any material copied from the work of another.

The editors expect all manuscripts to be submitted as an electronic Word document. Authors should submit one copy of the manuscript for books and two copies of manuscripts for articles on standard 8½-by-11 inch paper, double-spaced throughout, with the author's name on the title page only. They should follow the guidelines of *The Elements of Style* by William Strunk Jr. and E. B. White and consult the latest editions of *The Chicago Manual of Style* and *Merriam-Webster's Collegiate Dictionary*.

Authors should insert note numbers in the text, with notes appearing at the end of the complete text, not at the bottom of the page. The endnotes should document the sources on which a manuscript is based. IHS Press's staff carries out its long-standing tradition of checking text and notes for accuracy of facts and citations in manuscripts accepted for publication. Authors are responsible, however, for their own statements of fact or opinion.

The editors will consider manuscripts submitted by members of the IHS Board of Trustees and the editorial boards of the IHS Press and Family History Publications, but such manuscripts will be treated as those received from any other source and are subject to the criteria and procedures outlined in this policy statement. A trustee may be paid like any other author. An employee of IHS may be paid for a publication that is not written within the scope of his or her employment. A publication written by an employee within the scope of his or her employment by IHS—or written by a nonemployee who is paid by IHS for the creation of the publication—will be considered a work made for hire for which there is no additional compensation. All authors—whether employees or non-employees—shall sign a contract.

IHS Press does not publish fiction (except for children's books).

A rejected manuscript will be returned to the author upon request.

AUTHOR GUIDELINES FOR BOOKS FOR ADULTS

IHS Press seeks book-length publications about Indiana on topics such as—but not limited to—biography, personal narrative, immigration, family, cultural heritage, women, literature, folklore, music, the visual arts, politics, economics, industry, transportation, sports, geography, and military, medical, archaeological and agricultural history.

The editors require that manuscripts for potential publication be written in clear and appealing prose and in complete sentences free of jargon and undefined technical terms. Authors should avoid passive voice, lengthy quotations and one-sentence paragraphs.

The IHS Press will issue a standard contract to an author on acceptance of a book-length manuscript. The IHS Press shall own the copyright for books or book-length material that it finances and/or publishes. Submission of a manuscript by an author or receipt of a manuscript by IHS

Press should not in any way be construed as an obligation by IHS Press to publish a manuscript.

Please address all correspondence to:

Kathleen M. Breen
Editor, Indiana Historical Society Press
Eugene and Marilyn Glick Indiana History Center
450 West Ohio Street
Indianapolis, IN 46202-3269
(317) 232-1884
kbreen@indianahistory.org

AUTHOR GUIDELINES FOR CHILDREN'S BOOKS

IHS Press publishes at least one children's book per year. The press will consider manuscripts of well-researched nonfiction, particularly biographies, as well as manuscripts of fact-based historical fiction for children that are written in an engaging style with age-appropriate language and subject matter.

The main audiences for IHS Press children's books are students in grades kindergarten through twelve—and their educators and media specialists—with an emphasis on fourth grade and higher. Book selections for the children's book publishing program will provide content-rich resources related to Indiana history and the state's role in national and world events, identifying IHS Press as a reliable provider of excellent Indiana-related social studies literature.

Selections will be made based on the following general criteria: imaginative and engaging content, sound historical research, effective literary style and appropriateness for the audience. Ideally, the book will provide new knowledge about the topic or subject for students, incorporate a variety of primary and secondary sources and support the national and state educational standards for language arts and social studies.

The topics listed below are derived from curriculum standards for language arts and social studies. Manuscripts will be evaluated according to how well they fit within the time periods listed with the topics.

Topics for grades four and five

Indiana Territory, 1770s to 1816; Indiana statehood and development to the 1850s; Indiana in the Civil War Era; Indiana growth and development, 1880 to 1920; Indiana life, 1920 to the present. Topics with a focus on Indiana and the Midwest may also provide information on: America before and after the arrival of Europeans; American Indians and arrival of Europeans to 1770; American colonization and settlement; the

American Revolution; Creation of the United States Constitution and establishment of the Federal Republic, 1783 to 1800s.

Topics for grade eight

The following should be adapted with a focus on Indiana: Historical Time Period, 1750 to 1877: American Revolution and founding of the United States, 1754 to 1801; National Expansion and Reform, 1801 to 1861; Civil War and Reconstruction, 1850 to 1877.

Topics for High School

Early National Development, 1775 to 1877; Development of Industrial United States, 1870 to 1900; Emergence of Modern United States, 1897 to 1920; Modern United States, Prosperity and Depression, 1920 to 1940; United States and World War II, 1930 to 1945; Post-War United States, 1945 to 1960; United States in Troubled Times, 1960 to 1980; Contemporary United States, 1980 to present.

The IHS Press will issue a standard contract to an author on acceptance of a book-length manuscript. The Indiana Historical Society shall own the copyright in books or book-length material that it finances and/or publishes. Submission of a manuscript by an author or receipt of a manuscript by IHS Press should not in any way be construed as an obligation by IHS Press to publish a manuscript.

Address all correspondence to:

M. Teresa Baer
Managing Editor, Family History Publications
Indiana Historical Society Press
Eugene and Marilyn Glick Indiana History Center
450 West Ohio Street
Indianapolis, IN 46202-3269
(317) 234-0071
tbaer@indianahistory.org

AUTHOR GUIDELINES FOR *TRACES* MAGAZINE

The editors of *Traces* seek nonfiction articles that are solidly researched, attractively written and amenable to illustration, and they encourage scholars, journalists and freelance writers to contribute to the magazine. Accepted articles usually are a good mix of academic writing and magazine journalism.

IHS Press will issue a standard contract on acceptance of an article. IHS Press will hold a royalty-free exclusive license to publish the article in *Traces* — which converts to a royalty-free nonexclusive license six months after publication—and the right to permit Indiana newspapers to reprint the article. IHS Press owns the copyright in *Traces*, but the author owns the copyright in the article and is free to reprint the article after it is published in *Traces*. IHS Press is free to reprint the article at a future time.

Manuscript Guidelines

Traces seeks articles and essays on topics such as—but not limited to— biography, personal narrative, immigration, family, cultural heritage, women, literature, folklore, music, the visual arts, politics, economics, industry, transportation, sports, geography, and military, medical, archaeological, architectural and agricultural history. In addition, the magazine seeks essays from historians discussing their personal interest in the field of Indiana history.

In general, articles should be narrative in structure, have strong introductions and conclusions, and weave analysis into the larger framework. Essays should have a history component, preferably one that helps explain present practices, incidents and behaviors. The editors give priority to submissions that meet standards of research and presentation and also display a direct Indiana connection. Prospective authors should be familiar with the magazine before they submit articles or proposals.

Feature articles and essays should be 2,000 to 4,000 words in length. The editors primarily seek newly written material, although they will consider material that has been previously published. The editors will also respond to proposals submitted with writing samples and an indication of the means and costs of illustration.

Articles and essays should be written in clear and appealing prose that is free of jargon and undefined technical terms. Authors should avoid passive voice, lengthy quotations and one-sentence paragraphs. They should follow the guidelines of *The Elements of Style* by William Strunk Jr. and E. B. White and consult the latest editions of *The Chicago Manual of Style* and *Merriam-Webster's Collegiate Dictionary*.

Authors should submit two copies of each article or essay on standard 8½-by-11 inch paper, double-spaced throughout, with the author's name on the title page only. They should provide brief suggestions "For Further Reading" at the end of articles and document in endnotes the sources on which articles are based. The editors will decide the form and extent of published documentation. The editors accept approved manuscripts via e-mail.

Authors are responsible for providing illustrative material—in black and white or color—and captions that do not duplicate information in the text. IHS Press will provide staff assistance in locating—and will assume the cost of reproducing—photographs, maps and documents in the IHS collections. The quality and cost of potential illustration are major criteria by which the editors evaluate articles.

The editors initially review manuscripts submitted for publication, then send suitable ones to appropriate outside readers for evaluation. The editors make the final decision for or against publishing articles. Authors should allow 90 days or more for the evaluation process.

The editors reserve the right to copyedit accepted manuscripts to conform with the style and usage of *Traces*. The editorial staff checks the sources of articles to ensure accuracy of facts and citations. After editing an article, the editors will issue a standard contract and pay a negotiated honorarium to the author.

At the end of each volume year, the editorial board grants the Jacob Piatt Dunn Jr. Award, which includes a $500 prize, to the author whose article has best fulfilled the magazine's mission.

Manuscripts will be returned to authors if they are accompanied by a self-addressed envelope stamped with sufficient postage.

Address all correspondence to:

Ray Boomhower
Senior Editor, *Traces of Indiana and Midwestern History*
Indiana Historical Society Press
Eugene and Marilyn Glick Indiana History Center
450 West Ohio Street
Indianapolis, IN 46202-3269
(317) 232-1877
rboomhower@indianahistory.org

AUTHOR GUIDELINES FOR FAMILY HISTORY PUBLICATIONS

The editors of family history publications at the Indiana Historical Society Press publish research guidebooks and ethnic and immigration history books; the biannual family and local history journal *THG: Connections* and online publications that include book- and article-length indexes and source material that serve as keys for researchers into rare, archived material including—but not limited to—historic court records, business ledgers and personal journals. The editors of IHS Family History Publications seek nonfiction articles and book-length manuscripts that are solidly researched and attractively written, and they encourage genealogists, historians, journalists and freelance writers to make contributions.

Author Guidelines for Family History Books

The IHS Press's family history books include historical and genealogical research guides and ethnic and immigration histories.

IHS Press family history editors encourage scholars, journalists and freelance writers to contribute manuscripts that are solidly researched, attractively written, and amenable to illustration for family history books.

Family history books include: research guides about libraries, archives and other repositories and/or archived collections that would be highly useful for persons interested in Indiana and Midwestern history and/or genealogical research and histories or nonfiction stories of ethnic groups that live in Indiana including immigration stories. Topics may also include personal narrative, family, cultural heritage and folklore with a particular focus on providing historical context for genealogical research.

The editors require that manuscripts for potential publication be written in clear and appealing prose and in complete sentences free of jargon and undefined technical terms. Authors should avoid passive voice, lengthy quotations and one-sentence paragraphs.

The IHS Press will issue a standard contract to an author on acceptance of a book-length manuscript. IHS shall own the copyright in books or book-length material that it finances and/or publishes. Submission of a manuscript by an author or receipt of a manuscript by IHS Press should not in any way be construed as an obligation by IHS Press to publish a manuscript.

Address all correspondence to:

M. Teresa Baer
Managing Editor, Family History Publications
Indiana Historical Society Press
Eugene and Marilyn Glick Indiana History Center
450 West Ohio Street
Indianapolis, IN 46202-3269
(317) 234-0071
tbaer@indianahistory.org

AUTHOR GUIDELINES FOR *CONNECTIONS*

Connections is a family history journal of narrative articles on how to research, document, and write individual, family, and community history as well as histories of individuals, families, and communities.

The editors of *THG: Connections* seek nonfiction articles that are solidly researched, attractively written and amenable to illustration, and they encourage scholars, journalists, and freelance writers to contribute to the journal. Accepted articles usually combine information on how to research, document and/or write family history along with a story or stories discovered and pieced together from the author's own research.

The IHS Press will issue a standard contract on acceptance of an article and will pay a negotiated honorarium to the author. IHS Press will hold a royalty-free exclusive license to publish the article in *Connections* — which converts to a royalty-free nonexclusive license six months after publication. IHS Press owns the copyright in *Connections* but the author owns the copyright in the article and is free to reprint the article after it is published in *Connections*. IHS Press is free to reprint the article at a future time.

Manuscript Guidelines

Connections seeks articles and essays on topics such as—but not limited to—biography of individuals and/or families, personal narrative, immigration, cultural heritage, ethnic groups, women, folklore, geography, and military, medical, legal, archaeological, industrial, and agricultural history as these subjects provide historical context for genealogical research. In addition, we seek essays from genealogists and family historians discussing their personal experience in the field of family history research and writing on Indiana ancestors.

In general, articles should be narrative in structure, have strong introductions and conclusions and weave analysis into the larger framework. Essays should have both genealogy and history components, preferably ones that help explain present practices for family historians as well as incidents, behaviors and the historical environment of Indiana ancestors. The editors give priority to submissions that meet standards of research and presentation and also display a direct Indiana connection. Prospective authors should be familiar with the magazine before they submit articles or proposals.

Feature articles and essays should be 2,500 to 4,000 words in length. The editors primarily seek newly written material, although they will consider material that has been previously published. The editors will also respond to proposals submitted with writing samples and an indication of the means and costs of illustration.

Articles and essays should be written in clear and appealing prose that is free of jargon and undefined technical terms. Authors should avoid passive voice, lengthy quotations and one-sentence paragraphs. They should follow the guidelines of *The Elements of Style* by William Strunk Jr. and E. B. White and consult the latest editions of *The Chicago Manual of Style* and *Merriam-Webster's Collegiate Dictionary*.

Authors should submit two copies of each article or essay on standard 8½-by-11 inch paper, double-spaced throughout, with the author's name on the title page only. They should document their sources in endnotes. The editors will decide the form and extent of published documentation. A short biographical sketch of the author should also be included. The editors accept approved manuscripts via e-mail.

Authors are responsible for providing illustrative material—in black-and-white or color—and captions that do not duplicate information in the text. IHS Press will provide staff assistance in locating—and will assume the cost of reproducing—photographs, maps, and documents in the IHS collections.

The editors initially review manuscripts submitted for publication, then send suitable ones to appropriate outside readers for evaluation. The editors make the final decision for or against publishing articles. Authors should allow 90 days or more for the evaluation process.

The editors reserve the right to copyedit accepted manuscripts to conform with the style and usage of *Connections*. The editorial staff checks the sources of articles to ensure accuracy of facts and citations.

Authors of articles published in *Connections* may be nominated by the editors for the Willard C. Heiss Family History/Genealogy Award, given once each year by the Indiana Historical Society to "a family historian for his or her distinguished service and career in Indiana family history including presentations such as articles in *Connections*. . . ."

Manuscripts will be returned to authors if they are accompanied by a self-addressed envelope stamped with sufficient postage.

Address all correspondence to:

M. Teresa Baer
Managing Editor, Family History Publications
Indiana Historical Society Press
Eugene and Marilyn Glick Indiana History Center
450 West Ohio Street
Indianapolis, IN 46202-3269
(317) 234-0071
tbaer@indianahistory.org

AUTHOR GUIDELINES FOR *ONLINE CONNECTIONS*

Online Connections publishes indexes to rare source material and other database material helpful to genealogical and historical researchers looking for ancestors and other historic individuals including family genealogies.

The editors of IHS Press family history publications seek book- and article-length manuscripts on topics such as—but not limited to—name and vital statistics lists or other pertinent data from unpublished source material such as diaries, journals, ledgers, letter collections, and court, government, church, organizational, business and other records.

Prospective authors should be familiar with *Online Connections* publications before they submit manuscripts or proposals. Book-length manuscripts and article manuscripts submitted for the "Regional Sources and Stories," "Genealogy Across Indiana" and "Family Records" departments of *Online Connections* should include transcriptions and/or indexes of unpublished source material. These manuscripts should include introductions that describe the material, the historical background and repository of the source material and a guide describing the means of indexing and/or transcribing the material. Introductions should be no more than one to two pages in length and double spaced.

Transcriptions from original documents should reflect an exact replication of the passages transcribed, including capitalization, spelling, punctuation and grammar that would be considered incorrect in today's usage.

IHS Press will issue a standard contract on acceptance of an article. IHS Press will hold a royalty-free exclusive license to publish the article in *Online Connections*—which converts to a royalty-free nonexclusive license six months after publication. In the case of book-length publications, IHS Press will own the copyright in material that it finances and/or publishes. IHS Press owns the copyright in *Online Connections*, but the author owns the copyright in the article and is free to publish the article after it is published in *Online Connections*. IHS Press is free to publish the article at a future time.

Submission of a manuscript by an author or receipt of a manuscript by IHS Press should not in any way be construed as an obligation by IHS Press to publish a manuscript.

Manuscript Guidelines

The editors of *Online Connections* seek newly written material. The editors will also respond to proposals submitted with writing samples. Articles and essays should be written in clear and appealing prose that is free of jargon and undefined technical terms. Authors should avoid passive voice, lengthy quotations and one-sentence paragraphs. They should follow the guidelines of *The Elements of Style* by William Strunk Jr. and E. B. White and consult the latest editions of *The Chicago Manual of Style* and *Merriam-Webster's Collegiate Dictionary*.

Authors should submit two copies of each article or essay on standard 8½-by-11 inch paper, double-spaced throughout, with the author's name on the title page only. They should document their sources in endnotes. The editors will decide the form and extent of published documentation. A short biographical sketch of the author should also be included.

The editors accept article-length manuscripts via e-mail. Book-length manuscripts should be submitted on paper as stated above.

No illustrative material is required for *Online Connections* book-length publications and articles.

The editors initially review manuscripts submitted for publication, then send suitable ones to appropriate outside readers for evaluation. The editors make the final decision for or against publishing articles. Authors should allow 90 days or more for the evaluation process.

The editors reserve the right to copyedit accepted manuscripts to conform with the style and usage of *Online Connections*. The editorial staff checks the sources of articles to ensure accuracy of facts and citations.

Manuscripts for articles will be returned to authors if they are accompanied by a self-addressed envelope stamped with sufficient postage. Manuscripts for book-length publications will be returned upon request.

Address all correspondence to:

M. Teresa Baer
Managing Editor, Family History Publications
Indiana Historical Society Press Eugene and Marilyn Glick
Indiana History Center
450 West Ohio Street
Indianapolis, IN 46202-3269
(317) 234-0071
tbaer@indianahistory.org

Appendix 2: Sample Contract for an Article

Published with permission of the Indiana Historical Society Press.

AGREEMENT

This AGREEMENT is entered into by and between _____ (hereinafter referred to as the AUTHOR), a citizen of _____, whose address is _____, and the Indiana Historical Society Press (hereinafter referred to as the PRESS), a division of the Indiana Historical Society whose address is 450 West Ohio Street, Indianapolis, Indiana 46202-3269, for the publication of an article "_____" (hereinafter referred to as the ARTICLE) in *Traces of Indiana and Midwestern History* (hereinafter referred to as *TRACES*), a quarterly illustrated magazine.

In consideration of the mutual covenants and agreements set forth below and other valuable consideration, the sufficiency of which is hereby acknowledged, the parties hereto agree as follows:

1. *Author's Warranty:* The AUTHOR represents and warrants that he or she is the sole author of the ARTICLE; that he or she has full power and authority to make the AGREEMENT; that the ARTICLE does not infringe the copyright or other proprietary right of any other person; that it contains no libelous or other unlawful matter; that it makes no improper invasion of the privacy of any person; and that it has not been published previously in its present form.

2. *Author's Indemnification:* The AUTHOR agrees to defend the PRESS against any claim or action arising out of facts which constitute a breach of any of the representations and warranties set forth in paragraph 1 of this AGREEMENT and to indemnify and hold harmless the PRESS against any settlement or any final judgment for damages arising out of such claim or action, provided that the PRESS gives the AUTHOR prompt notice of any claim or action against the PRESS alleging facts which, if proved, could constitute a breach of these warranties. In the defense of any such claim or action, the AUTHOR may use counsel of his or her choosing, at the

AUTHOR's expense, and the PRESS may participate in the defense with counsel of the PRESS's choosing and at its expense. If any such claim or action is settled, or if there is a final judgment for damages arising out of any such claim or action, then the AUTHOR shall pay all reasonable costs and attorneys' fees incurred by the PRESS in defending such claim or action.

3. *Grants of License:* The AUTHOR grants to the PRESS a royalty-free exclusive license to reproduce and distribute (publish) copies of the ARTICLE in *TRACES* and on the PRESS's World Wide Web site (http://www.indianahistory.org), and the right to permit Indiana newspapers to reprint the ARTICLE in their newspapers. The PRESS shall own the copyright in *TRACES* and its Web site, but the AUTHOR retains ownership of the copyright in the ARTICLE. Six months after the ARTICLE is published in *TRACES*, the license granted herein to the PRESS shall automatically convert to a perpetual royalty-free nonexclusive license to publish copies of the ARTICLE as the PRESS chooses, in all print and electronic media, in a manner that may or may not include other portions of *TRACES*. Further, the AUTHOR shall thereafter be free to publish the ARTICLE elsewhere as he or she chooses. Once the license has become nonexclusive, the PRESS will refer to the AUTHOR requests from other publishers to reprint the ARTICLE, except AUTHOR agrees that all subsequent publication of the ARTICLE by the AUTHOR or by those to whom the AUTHOR has given permission must provide attribution to the PRESS and cite the volume and number of *TRACES* in which the ARTICLE was first published.

4. *Permission for Material:* If the ARTICLE incorporates any material (including, but not limited to, text, photographs, and illustrations) copied from a work by another, or any material copied from a previously published work by the AUTHOR, the AUTHOR shall acknowledge in the notes or captions of the WORK the source of such material and shall ascertain if permission is necessary to publish such material as part of the ARTICLE. If permission is necessary, the AUTHOR shall obtain such permission in writing from the owner of the copyright in such material. The PRESS shall pay fees for such permission, when required, subject to the approval of the PRESS's editor.

5. *Publishing Details:* The PRESS agrees to publish the ARTICLE in *TRACES* within one (1) year from the effective date of this AGREEMENT. If the PRESS has not published the ARTICLE within one year from the effective date, then the licenses granted to the PRESS in paragraph 3 above shall automatically convert to royalty-free nonexclusive licenses, and the AUTHOR shall thereafter be free to publish the ARTICLE elsewhere as he or she chooses. The PRESS

reserves the right to choose the issue of *TRACES* in which the ARTICLE will appear and to copyedit the ARTICLE to conform to the style and usage of *TRACES*. The AUTHOR will be given an opportunity to read the edited manuscript, but if he or she fails to return it to the editor of *TRACES* by the date set by the editor, production and publication will proceed without delay.

6. *Copies for Author:* The PRESS agrees to furnish the AUTHOR five (5) free copies of the issue of *TRACES* in which the ARTICLE is published at the time of printing. The AUTHOR shall also have the right to purchase additional copies of such issue of *TRACES* from the PRESS at a discount of fifty percent (50%) off the retail (non-members') price.

7. *Payment to Author:* As consideration for this AGREEMENT, the PRESS will pay the AUTHOR _____ dollars ($____).

8. *Choice of Law:* This AGREEMENT has been entered into in the State of Indiana and the validity, interpretation, and legal effect of this AGREEMENT shall be governed by the laws of Indiana.

9. *Entire Agreement:* This AGREEMENT sets forth the entire agreement between the parties with respect to the subject matter hereof, and this AGREEMENT supersedes all proposals or prior agreements, oral or written, and all other communications between the parties relating to the subject matter hereof. No modification, amendment, waiver, termination, or discharge of this AGREEMENT or any provision hereof shall be binding upon the PRESS unless confirmed in writing by an officer of the PRESS.

10. *Effective Date:* The effective date of this AGREEMENT is the date of the signature of the last party to sign and date this AGREEMENT.

If the foregoing terms are satisfactory, please sign and date this AGREEMENT, return one copy to the PRESS, and retain the second copy for your own files.

For the PRESS: AUTHOR:

_____   _____

Date: Date:

_____   _____

                                                 Social Security Number:

                                                 _____

Appendix 3: Sample Contract for a Book

Published with permission of the Indiana Historical Society Press.

AGREEMENT

This AGREEMENT is entered into by and between _____ (hereinafter referred to as the AUTHOR), a citizen of _____, whose address is _____, and the Indiana Historical Society Press (hereinafter referred to as the PRESS), a division of the Indiana Historical Society whose address is 450 West Ohio Street, Indianapolis, Indiana 46202-3269, for the publication of a work provisionally titled "_____" (hereinafter referred to as the WORK).

In consideration of the mutual covenants and agreements set forth and other valuable considerations, the sufficiency of which is hereby acknowledged, the parties hereto agree as follows:

1. *Author's Warranty:* The AUTHOR represents and warrants that he/she is the sole author of the WORK; that he/she has full power and authority to make this AGREEMENT; that the WORK does not infringe the copyright or other proprietary right of any other person; that it contains no libelous or other unlawful matter; that it makes no improper invasion of the privacy of any person; and that it has not been published previously in its present form.

2. *Author's Indemnification:* The AUTHOR agrees to defend the PRESS against any claim or action arising out of facts which constitute a breach of any of the representations and warranties set forth in paragraph 1 of this AGREEMENT and to indemnify and hold harmless the PRESS against any settlement or any final judgment for damages arising out of such claim or action, provided that the PRESS gives the AUTHOR prompt notice of any claim or action against the PRESS alleging facts which, if proved, could constitute a breach of those representations and warranties. In the defense of any such claim or action, the AUTHOR may use counsel of his/her choosing, at the AUTHOR's expense, and the PRESS may participate in the defense with counsel of the PRESS's choosing and at its

expense. If any such claim or action is settled, or if there is a final judgment for damages arising out of any such claim or action, then the AUTHOR shall pay all reasonable costs and attorneys' fees incurred by the PRESS in defending such claim or action.

3. *Assignment of Copyright:* The AUTHOR hereby assigns, sells, and conveys to the PRESS the entire rights, title and interests in and to the WORK, including the copyright therein and the right to sue for past infringements. The AUTHOR shall execute any document the PRESS deems necessary in connection with the assignment of the WORK and copyright therein, including the Assignment attached hereto as *Exhibit A.* The AUTHOR will take whatever steps and do whatever acts the PRESS requests, including, but not limited to, placement of the PRESS's proper copyright notice on the WORK to secure or aid in securing copyright protection in the WORK and will assist the PRESS or its nominees in filing applications to register claims of copyright in the WORK. The PRESS may file applications to register the copyright in the WORK as the copyright owner thereof.

4. *Permission for Material:* If the WORK incorporates any material (including, but not limited to, text, photographs, and illustrations) copied from a work by another, or any material copied from a previously published work by the AUTHOR, the AUTHOR shall acknowledge in the notes or captions of the WORK the source of such material and shall ascertain if permission is necessary to publish such material as part of the WORK. If permission is necessary, the AUTHOR shall obtain such permission in writing from the owner of copyright in such material. The PRESS shall pay fees for such permission, when required, subject to the approval of the PRESS's editor.

5. *Conflicting Publication:* The AUTHOR shall not, without the written permission of the PRESS, publish or permit to be published any material from the WORK and shall not create any derivative works based upon the WORK.

6. *Publishing Details:* The PRESS agrees to publish the WORK no later than _____. Should the PRESS fail to publish the WORK by _____, the assignment to the PRESS hereunder shall terminate at the option of the AUTHOR, and if such option is exercised by the AUTHOR, then all rights, title, and interests in the WORK including the copyright therein shall revert to the AUTHOR. If the PRESS fails to publish the WORK by _____, then such option may be exercised by the AUTHOR by posting a notice to that effect addressed to the PRESS by registered mail. The PRESS reserves the right to copyedit the WORK to conform to the style and usage of the PRESS's publications. The AUTHOR will be given an opportunity to read the edited manuscript, but if he/she fails to return it to

the PRESS's editor by the date set by the editor, production and publication will proceed without delay. The PRESS will coordinate the distribution of review copies and other complimentary copies of the WORK as it deems desirable in the interest of advertising the WORK.

7. *Copies for Author:* The PRESS shall furnish the AUTHOR ten (10) free copies of the WORK at the time of first printing. The AUTHOR shall have the right to purchase additional copies of the WORK from the PRESS at a discount of fifty percent (50%) off the retail (nonmembers') price. The AUTHOR may sell copies of the WORK if the PRESS provides the copies, receives the total revenue from the sale, and pays the AUTHOR royalties in accordance with paragraph 8 of this AGREEMENT; but the AUTHOR shall not sell copies of the WORK as a retailer and shall not resell copies of the WORK sold to him/her at the AUTHOR's discount.

8. *Payments to Author:* The PRESS shall pay to the AUTHOR, on sales of the WORK, six percent (6%) of the net revenue received on the sale of all copies of the WORK, but no payment shall be paid to the AUTHOR for copies of the WORK sold to the AUTHOR or distributed for review or for promotion. The PRESS will render statements of accounts annually as of December 31, and make payment within three months after December 31. No advance payment will be made by the PRESS to the AUTHOR.

9. *Promotional Appearances:* The AUTHOR agrees, after the publication of the WORK, to attend and to speak on the WORK at no less than six (6) book-signing events to promote the sale of the WORK, at no cost to the PRESS, except that the PRESS shall reimburse the AUTHOR at the PRESS's current standard reimbursement rate for mileage incurred for travel outside of (AUTHOR's home) County, Indiana; the number of trips to be reimbursed shall be subject to the approval of the PRESS's editor. Any additional expenses for which the AUTHOR seeks reimbursement will be addressed in a separate agreement.

10. *Choice of Law:* This AGREEMENT has been entered into in the State of Indiana and the validity, interpretation and legal effect of this AGREEMENT shall be governed by the laws of Indiana.

11. *Entire Agreement:* This AGREEMENT sets forth the entire agreement between the parties with respect to the subject matter hereof, and this AGREEMENT supersedes all proposals or prior agreements, oral or written, and all other communications between the parties relating to the subject matter hereof. No modification, amendment, waiver, termination, or discharge of this AGREEMENT or any provision hereof, shall be binding upon the PRESS unless confirmed in writing by an officer of the PRESS.

12. *Assignment and Successors:* This AGREEMENT and all the provisions hereof shall be binding upon and inure to the benefit of the parties hereto and their respective successors and permitted assigns, but neither this AGREEMENT nor any of the rights, interests or obligations hereunder shall be assigned by the AUTHOR without prior written consent of the PRESS. This AGREEMENT and any of the rights, interests, or obligations hereunder may be assigned by the PRESS.

13. *Effective Date:* The effective date of this AGREEMENT is the date of the signature of the last party to sign and date this AGREEMENT.

If the foregoing terms are satisfactory, please sign and date two copies of this AGREEMENT, return one copy to the PRESS, and retain the second copy for your own files.

For the PRESS: AUTHOR:

_____   _____

Date: Date:

_____   _____

                                 Social Security Number:

                                 _____

ASSIGNMENT

In consideration of valuable considerations including an AGREEMENT dated and effective _____, the receipt and sufficiency of which are hereby acknowledged, I, _____, a citizen of _____, whose address is _____, have assigned, sold and conveyed and do hereby assign, sell and convey to the Indiana Historical Society Press, 450 West Ohio Street, Indianapolis, Indiana 46202-3269, its successors and assigns, the entire rights, title, and interests in and to a work made for hire on _____ ("Work"), including the copyright in such WORK in the United States and all other countries of the world, as well as the right to sue for past infringements.

 IN WITNESS WHEREOF, I have executed this assignment at _____ this _____ day of _____.

AUTHOR:

_____

STATE OF _____

COUNTY OF _____

Subscribed and acknowledged before me this _____ day of _____.

_____
Notary Public

_____
Printed Name

My Commission Expires: _____, 20__.

Appendix 4: Sample Contract with a Photographer

Published with permission of the Indiana Historical Society Press.

AGREEMENT

This AGREEMENT is entered into by and between _____, (hereinafter referred to as the PHOTOGRAPHER), a citizen of _____, whose address is _____, and the Indiana Historical Society (hereinafter referred to as the SOCIETY), whose address is 315 West Ohio Street, Indianapolis, Indiana 46202-3299, for the publication of color photographs of _____ (hereinafter referred to as the PHOTOGRAPHS) in a publication tentatively titled "_____."

In consideration of the mutual covenants and agreements set forth below and other valuable consideration, the sufficiency of which is hereby acknowledged, the parties hereto agree as follows:

1. Photographer's Warranty: The PHOTOGRAPHER represents and warrants that he is the sole creator of the PHOTOGRAPHS; that he has full power and authority to make this Agreement; that the PHOTOGRAPHS do not infringe the copyright or other intellectual property rights of any other person; that they contain no libelous or other unlawful matter; that they make no improper invasion of the privacy of any person; and that they have not been published previously in their present form.

2. Photographer's Indemnification: The PHOTOGRAPHER agrees to defend the SOCIETY against any claim or action arising out of facts which constitute a breach of any of the representations and warranties set forth in paragraph 1 of this Agreement and to indemnify and hold harmless the SOCIETY against any settlement or any final judgment for damages arising out of such claim or action, provided that the SOCIETY gives the PHOTOGRAPHER prompt notice of any claim or action against the SOCIETY alleging facts which, if proved, could constitute a breach of these warranties. In the defense of any such claim or action, the PHOTOGRAPHER may use counsel of his or her choosing, at the PHOTOGRAPHER's expense, and the SOCIETY may participate in the defense with counsel of the SOCIETY's choosing and at its expense. If any such claim or action is settled, or if there is a final judgment for damages arising out of any such claim or action, then the PHOTOGRAPHER shall pay all reasonable costs and attorneys' fees incurred by the SOCIETY in defending such claim or action.

3. *Grant of License:* The PHOTOGRAPHER grants to the SOCIETY a royalty-free exclusive license to reproduce and distribute (publish) copies of the PHOTOGRAPHS. The SOCIETY shall own the copyright in the publication in which the PHOTOGRAPHS are published, but the PHOTOGRAPHER retains ownership of copyright in the PHOTO-GRAPHS. The SOCIETY will refer to the PHOTOGRAPHER requests from other publishers to reprint the PHOTOGRAPHS. One year after the PHOTOGRAPHS are published by the SOCIETY, the license granted herein to the SOCIETY shall automatically convert to royalty-free nonex-clusive license. The PHOTOGRAPHER shall thereafter be free to publish the PHOTOGRAPHS elsewhere as he chooses.

4. *Publishing Details:* The PHOTOGRAPHER shall deliver to the SOCI-ETY the finished PHOTOGRAPHS no later than _____. The SOCI-ETY agrees to publish the PHOTOGRAPHS within two (2) years from the effective date of this Agreement. If the SOCIETY has not published the PHOTOGRAPHS within two (2) years from the effective date, then the license granted to SOCIETY in paragraph 3 above shall automatically convert to a royalty-free nonexclusive license, and the PHOTOGRA-PHER shall thereafter be free to publish the PHOTOGRAPHS elsewhere as he chooses.

5. *Copies for Photographer:* The SOCIETY agrees to furnish the PHOTOGRAPHER three (3) free copies of the publication in which the WORK is published at the time of first printing. The PHOTOGRAPHER shall have the right to purchase from the SOCIETY additional copies of the publication in which the WORK is published at the members' price.

6. *Payment to Photographer:* As consideration for this Agreement, with-in thirty (30) days after receipt of the PHOTOGRAPHS by the SOCIETY's editor and Publications Division, the SOCIETY will pay the PHOTOG-RAPHER _____.

7. *Choice of Law:* This Agreement has been entered into in the State of Indiana and the validity, interpretation, and legal effect of this Agree-ment shall be governed by the laws of Indiana.

8. *Entire Agreement:* This Agreement sets forth the entire agreement between the parties with respect to the subject matter hereof, and this Agreement supersedes all proposals or prior agreements, oral or written, and all other communications between the parties relating to the subject matter hereof. No modification, amendment, waiver, termination, or dis-charge of this Agreement or any provision hereof shall by binding upon the SOCIETY unless confirmed in writing by an officer of SOCIETY.

9. *Effective Date:* The effective date of this Agreement is the date of the signature of the last party to sign and date this Agreement.

If the foregoing terms are satisfactory, please sign and date this Agreement, return one copy to the SOCIETY, and retain the second copy for your own files.

For the SOCIETY: PHOTOGRAPHER:

_____   _____

Date: Date:

_____   _____

Social Security Number:

_____

Appendix 5: Sample Request for Proposal for Typesetting and Printing a Journal

The original of this request for proposal (with details of date and recipient here removed) resulted in the typesetting and printing of *Documentary Editing*, the quarterly journal of the Association for Documentary Editing.

As we have discussed, I would like Typesetting Company, Inc., to provide me with an estimate of expenses for typesetting, printing, and mailing *Documentary Editing* during the calendar year ____. In general, you can use the previous issues that Typesetting Company produced in ____ [year] as a model. I have organized the categories of specifications (especially numbers 10–13) to coincide with the categories that you currently use in billing the Association for Documentary Editing (ADE). I will need the estimate no later than 23 October, which is the day before I leave for the ADE annual meeting, where I will present the estimates to the Council. I will FAX you this letter, with hard copy to follow by mail.

1. *Item: Documentary Editing*, the journal of the Association for Documentary Editing (ADE).
2. *Frequency*: Quarterly (March, June, September, and December).
3. *Schedule*: Typesetting Company to provide a production schedule for each issue during the calendar year ____.
4. *Trim size*: 8 1/2 x 11 inches.
5. *Paper*: Typesetting Company or its subcontractor to supply 70-pound one-color acid-free coated (matte) text stock and 80-pound two-color acid-free coated (matte) cover stock.
6. *Ink*: Black and one PMS color.
7. *Binding*: Saddle-stitched on the 11-inch side.
8. *Billing*: ADE is the fiscal agent. Bills will be sent to me at the above address; I will approve payment and send the bills to the ADE treasurer for payment.
9. *Pages*: Text, 24 pages, black-and-white on both sides; plus cover black-and-white inside and two-color outside. With typesetting and printing quotes, please also indicate additional cost for 28 text pages and 32 text pages.

10. *Typesetting and Page Makeup*: ADE will supply diskettes containing all text, with typesetting codes input using the codes specified by Typesetting Company in _____ [year]. Typesetting Company supplies galley proofs, from which ADE will make up rough dummy pages. Typesetting Company will supply page proofs. Please quote base price for typesetting and page makeup, unit cost of alterations, and hourly cost of page makeup alterations.

11. *Illustrations*: ADE will supply illustrations. Please quote unit cost for halftones and screen tints.

12. *Printing*: Typesetting Company or its subcontractor will provide silverprints (blues). Quote printing cost for 550 copies base press-run. Also quote per-copy price above 550. Please state policy on percent over or under pressrun.

13. *Mailing*: ADE to supply pressure-sensitive labels, sorted in ZIP code order. Typesetting Company or its subcontractor to supply 9 x 12-inch envelopes printed with return address and postal permit information, affix labels, insert the journal in the envelopes, deliver envelopes containing journals to the post office, and deliver overage to the editor of the journal in Indianapolis, Indiana. Please quote unit cost to stuff, label, sort, and mail the journal. Also quote cost of envelopes.

If you need further information in preparing this estimate, please call me.

Yours sincerely,
Thomas A. Mason
Editor

Appendix 6: Sample Request for Proposals for Writing a Book

This request for proposals resulted in the writing of E. Bruce Geelhoed, *The Rotary Club of Indianapolis: A Club, a Community, and a Century, 1913–1998* (Carmel: Guild Press of Indiana, 2000).

REQUEST FOR PROPOSALS FOR WRITING A NEW HISTORY OF THE ROTARY CLUB OF INDIANAPOLIS

The Rotary Club of Indianapolis seeks proposals to write a history of the club.

Purpose: The purpose of the history of the Rotary Club of Indianapolis will be:

- to orient new members to the background of our organization.
- to increase an understanding of the club among our existing membership and, to whatever extent possible, the wider reading public.

Several preliminary tasks must be undertaken as part of the background research, as follows:

- A questionnaire has been drafted to be circulated to all club members, asking them if they have recollections or records (papers, pamphlets, minutes, photographs, or other audiovisual materials) that would be useful for this project. A form of the questionnaire must be submitted to the 650 members.
- Oral history interviews need to be conducted with older members whose recollections will be important to the history. The interviews could be conducted by the author or by other persons, but all interviewers should receive some basic training in oral history interviewing techniques. Signed release forms need to be obtained from the interviewees. We should come up with a pattern for those interviews. History Committee members are willing to conduct oral history interviews. The History Committee can be expanded to include more people who will conduct those interviews.
- Club records dating back to 1913 are deposited in a storeroom on the sixth floor of the Indianapolis Athletic Club, down the corridor from the Rotary office. These records need to be processed and

organized, and a basic guide or finding aid needs to be created. A History Committee member has made an initial inventory—which is printed on the reverse side of this request for proposals—of the records in the storeroom. Depending on the skills and experience of the author, we might contract separately with a person or organization to process and organize the collection. The History Committee has recommended that, after the history project is completed, the Board of Directors place the club records (including photographs) in a professionally staffed archive where they can be well cared for. If any records turn out to have no archival value, the person working on the collection could make recommendations to the Board of Directors concerning the disposition of such records.

TIMELINE

1997: History Committee searches for author to write the book and a person to organize the records (who might or might not be the same person). We hope to make a selection in June.

1997–1998: Records are organized. Author conducts research and writing. History to be complete prior to the international meeting in Indianapolis, 14–17 June 1998. The author will then attend and write an account of the international meeting, and make that the book's concluding event. The goal is to bring the book out in late 1998 or early 1999.

We seek an author with the following profile:

- a proven ability to organize a research project and carry it to a successful conclusion
- a writing style that will engage a wide audience
- knowledge of recent Indiana history and its documentation
- an established publication record is highly desirable

GENERAL INFORMATION

Proposals should include a narrative specifying the project director's plan and how it will be implemented, a budget including all costs (including provision for transcription of approximately thirty oral history interviews), and résumés of persons who will be involved with the project. Persons making proposals may request an inspection copy of John McDowell's *From Flood to Fire: The History of Indianapolis Rotary Club, 1913–1969* (1969). Proposals received by 31 May are assured consideration, but the search will continue until a selection is made. Proposals should be sent to the chair of the History Committee: Thomas A. Mason, Indiana Historical Society, 315 West Ohio Street, Indianapolis, Indiana

46202–3299; phone (317) 232-6546; fax (317) 233-3109; E-mail tmason @statelib.lib.in.us.

The History Committee will create teasers on the history project to appear in the club's newsletter. A short brochure on our club should be created as a spin-off from the book project.

From Flood to Fire contains approximately 80,000 words of text plus 72 illustrations in 251 pages, plus three appendixes. The appendixes cover current members, past members, and other Indiana Rotary Clubs and their charter dates. A full list of past members is not feasible today because of large numbers, but the new history will include appendixes on past officers and other Indiana Rotary Clubs and their charter dates. It will also include an index, a feature not in *From Flood to Fire*. The History Committee has recommended that a long-term plan be developed to produce ongoing supplements every decade.

The history will be a fully integrated, stand-alone study to replace *From Flood to Fire*, to be somewhat shorter and less detailed than that earlier book, stressing broad themes, and covering from the club's founding in 1913 through the Rotary International Convention here in Indianapolis in June 1998. For the years already covered by *From Flood to Fire*, the author of the new history will be charged to edit and condense material from the earlier book, the copyright of which the club owns. The contract will call for the author to deliver a typescript of 200–250 pages or approximately 64,000 words. At least one chapter will be devoted to the 1998 Rotary International Convention.

Appendix 7: Sample Request for Proposals for Publishing a Book

This request for proposals resulted in the publication of E. Bruce Geelhoed, *The Rotary Club of Indianapolis: A Club, a Community, and a Century, 1913–1998* (Carmel: Guild Press of Indiana, 2000).

REQUEST FOR PROPOSALS FOR PUBLICATION OF A NEW HISTORY OF THE ROTARY CLUB OF INDIANAPOLIS

The Rotary Club of Indianapolis seeks proposals for publication of a book on the history of the club. Responsibilities will include production—design, production coordination, prepress (typesetting and page makeup), printing, binding, and marketing/publishing/distribution. The club also seeks proposals to produce a color brochure for marketing the book. The goal is to bring the book out in late 1998 or early 1999.

Written by E. Bruce Geelhoed, professor of history at Ball State University and director of the Center for Middletown Studies, the book is tentatively titled "A Club, a Community, and a Century: The Rotary Club of Indianapolis, 1913–1998." It will have the following elements and chapters: Introduction; 1. The Formative Years, 1913–1919; 2. The Emergence of a Community Identity, 1920–1929; 3. The Rotary Club amidst the Depression, 1930–1939; 4. The War Years and Postwar Resurgence, 1940–1949; 5. Strengthening the Roots in the Community, 1950–1959; 6. A New Surge of Activism, 1960–1969; 7. The Rotary Club as a Mature Organization, 1970–1979; 8. The Rotary Club Faces the Challenges of Growth, 1980–1989; 9. A Fixture in the Community, 1990–1998; 10. The 1998 Rotary International Convention in Indianapolis; Conclusion.

The vendor(s) will provide:

- Design and printing a color brochure for marketing the book, incorporating an order form for the book, 2,000 copies, to be produced by 5 June.
- A finished book with the following specifications:
  Rotary will provide, by 1 September 1998, a typescript and computer disk with Macintosh-generated text of the book (including index), and glossy photographs for illustrations. The text delivered by Rotary will have been edited by a member of Rotary who is an

experienced copyeditor. For purposes of cost estimates, assume: a typescript of 200 pages or 64,000 words, 100 halftone illustrations, 6 x 9-inch cover size, and a pressrun of 1,500 copies printed on acid-free paper. Binding: Please quote three ways (1) a 2-color paper cover; (2) 4-color paper cover; (3) split pressrun of 500 clothbound copies with 4-color jacket, and 1,000 copies with 4-color paper cover.

- Marketing/advertising/distribution for the book.

These services will not necessarily all be provided by the same vendor.

Proposals should state the estimated cost for the service to be provided. Proposals received by 19 May are assured consideration, but the search will continue until a selection is made. Proposals should be sent to the chair of the Rotary History Committee: Thomas A. Mason, Indiana Historical Society, 315 West Ohio Street, Indianapolis, Indiana 46202-3299; phone (317) 232-6546; fax (317) 233-3109; E-mail tmason @statelib.lib.in.us.

Appendix 8: Why Books Cost: A Quick Lesson in Finance for Publishers

Gregory M. Britton, Editorial Director, Johns Hopkins University Press

Publishing any book involves a certain amount of speculation. Whether publishing an e-book or a print one, before a publisher can recover any money, there has to be a book to sell. To get that book the publisher must first select, edit, design, typeset, and manufacture it. Authors, unless they are fortunate enough to command high advances against royalties, also do their work only with the hope it will be published and that they may earn royalties on sales. This speculation is at the very heart of publishing. It is even true for the nonprofit publisher which may have grant money to support publication, but still needs to limit possible losses. Most institutions want to publish books that advance their mission, but they must do this in a financially prudent way.

Publishers, especially small ones or those new to the business, are prone to a common pitfall in planning their book projects. Swept up in the enthusiasm of a book idea or coming celebration, a historical society can underestimate the cost of publishing and overestimate the interest of potential book buyers. This enthusiasm, at once essential for gathering support and getting the work done, can be disastrous if it drives financial planning and print decisions. Publishers should direct the enthusiasm to promoting the forthcoming book, but keep a steely eye on the book budget. If you are wrong and the market responds with vigor, you can always make more quickly. This is a much better situation than being stuck with a back room filled with pallets of unwanted books.

Any organization planning to publish a book should begin with a basic budget that summarizes the potential income a book will generate and the potential expenses it will take to make that book. This tool—a simple profit-and-loss statement (or P&L)—can also be used to test certain assumptions about the project. What happens if you raise book's list price 10 percent? What happens if you obtain a subsidy or grant of $5,000? The P&L can be a powerful planning tool. Publishers create these for every project and often for their entire list of forthcoming projects.

Appendix 8

SAMPLE PROFIT AND LOSS STATEMENT

Author/Title	Smith / *Two Centuries of Us*
Binding:	Hardcover
Page Count:	240 pp
Illustration Count	30 black & white photos
Royalty Rate	5.0%

SALES INCOME	
List price	$29.95
Print quantity	2,000
Discount	50%
Ave. receipts	$14.98
Comps and frees	100
Copies to sell	1,900
TOTAL INCOME	$28,462

COST OF SALES	
Editorial costs	$2,300
Prepress costs	$5,900
Manufacturing costs	$14,535
Royalty expense	$1,423
Expense subtotal	$24,158

Unit cost	$12.08
Subsidy	-$8,000
TOTAL COST	$16,158

GROSS MARGIN	$12,304
PERCENT MARGIN	43.2%
UNITS TO BREAK EVEN	1,080

The profit-and-loss statement should be created early in a project's planning and updated as decisions are made about the book, its physical characteristics like size, binding, and number of illustrations, and its potential market. Since the P&L only records assumptions or best guesses about what might happen, so as assumptions change so should the book's budget. As you incur actual expenses (a copyediting bill, for example), the P&L can be updated and rechecked.

The top section of the P&L records some fixed aspects of the book—its author and title, binding, and page and illustration counts—that you will need to obtain prices for manufacturing. Changes to these, a higher number of pages or a change in the number of illustrations, will affect the prices below.

The next section on the P&L calculates the income side of our equation. We have priced our sample book at $29.95, and we hope to print two thousand copies. Since books sold through trade stores, both online and brick-and-mortar, require substantial discounting from the publisher, our P&L assumes a 50 percent average discount. Books sold directly to a buyer might command full price, but it is best to assume the worst for budgeting. The average income for that $29.95 book, then, is only $14.98.

Promoting books—sending complimentary books to reviewers and media—requires distributing some free copies. This is common in book publishing and we need to plan for this. We may also owe the author some free copies according to the contract. The P&L assumes we will give away 100 books at no charge, leaving us 1,900 to sell at $14.98, or $28,462.

The third portion of the P&L collects the costs associated with the project. This one separates them into editorial costs like copyediting, proofreading, indexing, and permissions fees. Prepress expenses include any costs involved in preparing the manuscript for either manufacturing as a print or e-book, like design, composition, art scanning, and file conversion. Manufacturing costs involve the actual paper, printing, binding, and shipping books to the warehouse, the total bill expected from the printer. For our purposes, it matters less which category an expense falls into than that *all* expenses are accounted for on the spreadsheet.

Some publishers also assign an expense line in this section for institutional overhead costs. This recognizes that there are certain expenses that are not a direct cost of the project but nevertheless must be borne by it. Overhead costs, for example, include rent and utilities, staff expenses, equipment costs. The P&L totals all expense and divides that by the total print quantity to give a unit cost, in this case $12.08 per book. So every book we manufacture will cost us $12.08.

It is likely that regional history books will be subsidized in some way. Their markets, bound by geography, are naturally finite. Because these books are often discretionary purchases, their prices are usually lower than, say, textbooks or professional reference books. The P&L subtracts any grant money for the project from the costs of sales. Why is a subsidy not counted in the income section since technically it is income? Remember that we calculate author royalties on total *sales* income and do not want to elevate the income number with grant dollars.

The final part of the P&L calculates a few different and useful metrics. The first is gross profit margin—simply total income minus total cost. In the case of our example, it is $12,304. Second, we calculate percent gross profit margin, which is gross profit margin divided by total income. This gives us the profit as a percent of income. Here it is just over 43 percent. As a rule of thumb, a publisher should strive to get this number as high as possible—since it is a measure of how efficient a book is at generating a profit—and may be reluctant to take on projects with a percent margin much below 60 percent.

The last calculation is simply the number of books we must sell to break even, calculated by dividing total costs by average receipts. In our example, we only begin to earn anything after we sell the first 1,080 books.

These indicators are tools that help publishers make decisions and monitor progress. They are based on certain assumptions, however, the most striking of which is that except for the books you plan to give away, you hope to sell every copy. Another is that your average discount and average receipt are accurate estimates. And finally, that the prepress and print vendors have correctly estimated their prices.

The best example of how the P&L becomes a decision-making tool comes in testing "what if" scenarios. The original P&L, for example, assumed a book that would sell 1,900 copies. What would happen if we could sell 2,900? What would our added expenses be and what would be our resulting income?

SCENARIO PLANNING

The first column of figure 2 (see the following page) shows the budgeted scenario while the second column tests what would happen if we sold a thousand more books. Obviously manufacturing costs go up but fixed costs like editorial and prepress remain the same. The unit cost falls and the gross profit margin improves significantly. Clearly, it is a better financial picture *if* we really can sell those extra books.

For comparison, the second scenario keeps the print run at two thousand, but increases the price by ten dollars resulting in a higher average receipt and more income. Costs remain the same, obviously, since we are not making more books, except for royalty expense which climb in relation to sales. Here too the gross profit margin is much improved, and, because we are selling books for more money, we have to sell fewer to break even.

What if we could find another donor and raise more subsidy? Scenario 3 follows the budget for quantity and price, but increases the subsidy. The final scenario raises both the price and the subsidy to very positive effect. Both profit margin and percent profit are the highest of the scenarios, and we have to sell the lowest number before beginning to earn a profit.

Author / Title Smith/*Two Centuries of Us*

	Budgeted	Scenario 1	Scenario 2	Scenario 3	Scenario 4
SALES INCOME					
List price	$29.95	$29.95	$39.95	$29.95	$39.95
Quantity	2,000	3,000	2,000	2,000	2,000
Discount	50%	50%	50%	50%	50%
Ave. receipts	$14.98	$14.98	$19.98	$14.98	$19.98
Comps and frees	100	100	100	100	100
Copies to sell	1,900	2,900	1,900	1,900	1,900
TOTAL INCOME	$28,462	$43,428	$37,953	$28,462	$37,953
COST OF SALES					
Editorial costs	$2,300	$2,300	$2,300	$2,300	$2,300
Prepress costs	$5,900	$5,900	$5,900	$5,900	$5,900
Manufacturing costs	$14,535	$19,076	$14,535	$14,535	$14,535
Royalty expense	$1,423	$2,171	$1,897	$1,423	$1,897
Expense subtotal	$24,158	$29,447	$24,632	$24,158	$24,632
Unit cost	$12.08	$9.81	$12.96	$12.08	$12.96
Subsidy	-$8,000	-$8,000	-$8,000	-$10,000	-$10,000
TOTAL COST	$16,158	$21,447	$16,632	$14,158	$14,632
GROSS MARGIN	$12,304	$21,981	$21,321	$14,304	$23,321
PERCENT MARGIN	43.2%	50.6%	56.2%	50.3%	61.4%
UNITS TO BREAK EVEN	1,080	1,432	833	945	733

The value of this type of planning is that it allows you to test certain ideas before committing to them. Here we assumed that we could raise the price ten dollars and not harm unit sales. Would the same be true if we raised the price by fifteen? The danger in using this tool uncritically is that it can trick you into making risky choices. The most seductive is the lure of the larger press run where unit costs fall and potential profits soar, and the risk is that you end up with a mountain of unsold books. A more prudent course is to take a more calculated risk and print low. You can always print more if you were wrong.

Relying on good financial data does not eliminate the risks associated with publishing, but it does help you make sound decisions while understanding their consequences.

Bibliography

Ambrosius, Lloyd E., ed. *Writing Biography: Historians and Their Craft*. Lincoln: University of Nebraska Press, 2004.

Association of American University Presses and Joyce Kachergis, eds. *One Book/Five Ways: The Publishing Procedures of Five University Presses*. 1978; 2nd ed., Chicago: University of Chicago Press, 1994.

Beasley, David R. *Beasley's Guide to Library Research*. Toronto: University of Toronto Press, 2000.

Bailey, Herbert S., Jr. *The Art and Science of Book Publishing*. 1970; 3rd ed., Athens: Ohio University Press, 1990.

Barlow, Jeffrey G. "Historical Research and Electronic Evidence: Problems and Promises." In *Writing, Teaching, and Researching History in the Electronic Age: Historians and Computers*, edited by Dennis A. Trinkle, 194–225. Armonk, N.Y.: M. E. Sharpe, 1998.

Barzun, Jacques, and Henry F. Graf. *The Modern Researcher*. 1957; 6th ed., Belmont, Calif.: Thomson/Wadsworth Publishing, 2004.

Beckett, John. *Writing Local History*. Manchester, U.K.: Manchester University Press, 2007.

Benedict, Michael Les. *A Historian's Guide to Copyright*. Washington, D.C.: American Historical Association, 2012.

Bielstein, Susan M. *Permissions: A Survival Guide*. Chicago: University of Chicago Press, 2006.

Cohen, Daniel, and Roy Rosenzweig. *Digital History: A Guide to Gathering, Preserving, and Presenting the Past on the Web*. Philadelphia: University of Pennsylvania Press, 2005.

Collins, M. H. *Write History Right: How to Research, Organize, and Document the Past for Your Hometown, Region, Family, Sports Team, School, Events, Organization, Church: A Step-by-Step Guide*. Rogers, Ark.: CHS Publishing, 2009.

Cook, Tony. "Self-Publishing Comes in from the Cold with Sale." *Indianapolis Star*, July 20, 2012, A-5.

Felt, Thomas E. *Researching, Writing, and Publishing Local History*. 1976; 2nd ed., Nashville, Tenn.: American Association for State and Local History, 1981.

Fiering, Norman. *A Guide to Book Publication for Historians*. Washington, D.C.: American Historical Association, 1979.

Fischer, David Hackett. *Historians' Fallacies: Toward a Logic of Historical Thought*. New York: Harper & Row, 1970.

Germano, William. *Getting It Published: A Guide for Scholars and Anyone Else Serious about Serious Books*. 2001; 2nd ed., Chicago: University of Chicago Press, 2008.

Greco, Albert, Clara Rodríguez, and Robert Wharton. *The Culture and Commerce of Publishing in the 21st Century*. Stanford, Calif.: Stanford Business Books, 2007.

Harman, Eleanor, Ian Montagnes, Siobhan McMenemy, and Chris Bucci, eds. *The Thesis and the Book: A Guide for First-Time Academic Authors*. 1976; 2nd ed., Toronto: University of Toronto Press, 2003.

Kammen, Carol. *On Doing Local History*. 1986; 2nd ed., Walnut Creek, Calif.: AltaMira Press, 2003.

Kammen, Carol, and Amy H. Wilson, eds., *Encyclopedia of Local History*. 2000; 2nd ed. Lanham, Md.: AltaMira Press, 2013.

Kirsch, Jonathan. *Kirsch's Guide to the Book Contract: For Authors, Publishers, Editors, and Agents*. Los Angeles: Acrobat Books, 1999.

————. *Kirsch's Handbook of Publishing Law: For Authors, Publishers, Editors, and Agents.* 1995; Los Angeles: Silman-James Press, 2005.

Krug, Steve. *Don't Make Me Think: A Common Sense Approach to Web Usability.* 2000; 2nd ed., Berkeley, Calif.: New Riders, 2006.

Kyvig, David E., and Myron A. Marty. *Nearby History: Exploring the Past around You.* 1982; 3rd ed., Lanham, Md.: AltaMira Press, 2010.

Lee, Marshall. *Bookmaking: Editing/Design/Production.* 1965; 3rd ed., New York: Norton, 2004.

Luey, Beth E. *Handbook for Academic Authors.* 1987; 5th ed., New York: Cambridge University Press, 2010.

————, ed. *Revising Your Dissertation: Advice from Leading Editors.* 2004; 4th ed., Berkeley: University of California Press, 2011.

Lynch, Patrick J., and Sarah Horton. *Web Style Guide: Basic Design Principles for Creating Web Sites.* 1999; 3rd ed., New Haven, Conn.: Yale University Press, 2009.

Mann, Thomas. *The Oxford Guide to Library Research.* 1987; 3rd ed., New York: Oxford University Press, 2005.

Marius, Richard, and Melvin E. Page. *A Short Guide to Writing about History.* 1989; 8th ed., Boston: Pearson, 2012.

Mason, Thomas A. "Partnerships in Publications." *History News* 47, no. 4 (1992): 12–14, 32.

McLean, Gavin. *How to Do Local History: Research, Write, Publish: A Guide for Historians and Clients.* Dunedin, N.Z.: Otago University Press, 2007.

Morville, Peter, and Louis Rosenfeld. *Information Architecture for the World Wide Web: Designing Large-Scale Web Sites.* 1998; 3rd ed., Sebastopol, Calif.: O'Reilly Media, 2007.

Park, Karin R., and Beth E. Luey. *Publication Grants for Authors and Publishers: How to Find Them, Win Them, and Manage Them.* Phoenix, Ariz.: Oryx Press, 1991.

Parker, Donald Dean. *Local History: How to Gather It, Write It, and Publish It.* Revised and edited by Bertha E. Josephson for the Committee on Guide for Study of Local History of the Social Science Research Council. New York: SSRC, 1944.

Phillips, Lori Byrd, and Dominic McDevitt-Parks. "Historians in *Wikipedia*: Building an Open, Collaborative History." *Perspectives in History: The Newsmagazine of the American Historical Association* 50, no. 9 (December 2012): 55–56.

Posner, Richard A. *The Little Book of Plagiarism.* New York: Pantheon, 2007.

Presnell, Jenny L. *The Information-Literate Historian: A Guide to Research for History Students.* 2007; 2nd ed., New York: Oxford University Press, 2013.

Samuels, Edward. *The Illustrated Story of Copyright.* New York: Thomas Dunne Books, 2000.

Storey, William Kelleher. *Writing History: A Guide for Students.* 1999; 4th ed., New York: Oxford University Press, 2013.

Trinkle, Dennis A., and Scott A. Merriman, eds. *The American History Highway: A Guide to Internet Resources on U.S., Canadian, and Latin American History.* Armonk, N.Y.: M. E. Sharpe, 2007.

Trubshaw, Bob. *How to Write and Publish Local and Family History Successfully: Books, Booklets, Magazines, CD-ROMs, and Web Sites.* Loughborough, U.K.: Heart of Albion Press, 2005.

[Williams, Roger Lloyd]. *Self-Publishing: Planning for a Better Book.* 1983; Nappanee, Ind.: Evangel Press, 1992.

AASLH Technical Leaflets are available from the AASLH website (www.aaslh.org/leaflets. htm) in downloadable copy or hard copy. These are dated on the technology of printing, but the fundamental principles of publishing books on state and local history remain unchanged:

007 Warner, Sam Bass, Jr. *Writing Local History: The Use of Social Statistics.* 1970.

034 Walklet, John J., Jr. *Publishing in the Historical Society.* 1966.

039 Derby, Charlotte S. *Reaching Your Public: The Historical Society Newsletter.* 1967.

051 Alderson, William T. *Marking and Correcting Copy for Your Printer.* 1969.

053 Gore, Gary. *Spotting Mechanical Errors in Proof: A Guide for Linecasting Machine Proofreaders.* 1969.

103 Gore, Gary. *Phototypesetting: Getting the Most for Your Money.* 1978.

142 Purcell, L. Edward. *Writing Printing Specifications: A Systematic Approach to Publications Management.* 1981.

145 Enstam, Elizabeth Y. *Using Memoirs to Write Local History.* 1982.

Index

About the Authors

Thomas A. Mason is adjunct lecturer in history at Indiana University–Purdue University Indianapolis.

J. Kent Calder is the executive director of the Texas State Historical Association, located on the campus of the University of North Texas, Denton.